Drone Regulations in South Africa

Drone Regulations in South Africa

Philippe-Joseph Salazar

Drone Regulations in South Africa

First published 2025

Juta and Company (Pty) Ltd
First Floor, Sunclare Building, 21 Dreyer Street, Claremont 7708
PO Box 14373, Lansdowne 7779, Cape Town, South Africa
www.juta.co.za

© 2025 Juta and Company (Pty) Ltd

ISBN: 978 1 48515 471 6 (print)
ISBN: 978 1 48515 472 3 (epub)

Production specialist: Elvis Dyosi
Cover designer: Drag and Drop
Editor: Linda van de Vijver
Indexer: Sanet le Roux
Typesetter: Elinye Ithuba DTP Solutions

Typeset in Adobe Garamond Pro Regular 12/14pt

Printed and bound:

The author and the publisher believe on the strength of due diligence exercised that this work does not contain any material that is the subject of copyright held by another person. In the alternative, they believe that any protected pre-existing material that may be comprised in it has been used with appropriate authority or has been used in circumstances that make such use permissible under the law.

Table of Contents

Before We Take Off

This guide on the do's and don'ts of flying a civilian drone legally is intended for several groups of drone flyers:

➠ Drone enthusiasts who are interested in **flying drones for fun**, 'privately', and who are unsure of what is legal and what is not – not only because they fear a police van stopping outside, but because they want to be safe and make the most of it. This guide definitely tells the private drone flyer what to do, and what not to do: see section 2.

➠ Drone enthusiasts **who want a remote pilot licence** to start a job or even to set up a trade, and need sound advice about what it means to fly drones 'commercially': see sections 3 and 4.

➠ **Legal eagles** will find it useful. As I have supervised lawyers getting Master's and PhDs in air law, I am aware that, unless you are a pilot, the details of flying and aviation rules go over your head. Quite a few aviation law websites or 'guides' are outdated, or vague. (After all, why should a law firm give you, free of charge, the nitty gritty of flying drones legally?)

➠ **Drone operators**, flight schools, businesses and service providers should find it valuable, unless they are already in the game. However, someone starting up in one of the trades associated with drones – land surveying, photography, the film industry and security – needs to have a clear idea about how to become an operator in terms of state regulations. Section 6 is for them.

➠ **Drone pilot trainees** will also find it valuable. If you are studying to become a drone pilot proper, this pocketbook can double up as a quick reference guide. Due to South African Civil Aviation Authority (SACAA) rules about training and awarding licences, this guide will not replace formal instruction at a flight school. Aspiring drone pilots must get through compulsory enrolment and study at a flight school, with experienced certified instructors. But this guide can be used to prepare you to make your move to enrol at a flight school and get a fair idea of what is in store.

➠ **Foreign visitors** who may or may not bring their own drones. South Africa is a choice destination: you can fly two Classes of drones privately: see section 2. Do not try to do commercial filming on the sly, unless you are an operator: see section 6. FPV drone flying is forbidden.

How much must you know about flying?

It depends. Some readers will have no idea of what aviation involves, and some may well be licensed pilots already. So, some explanations may sound a bit banal to aviators or even obvious to newcomers who think they know about the subject. But, in aviation, nothing is obvious. And there are plenty of rules. Let me use a fun dialogue to illustrate what is 'obvious':

- An aerial drone flies.
- Obvious!
- Then, it is an aircraft.
- Well, yes, but, okay, obvious.
- This one you are holding, what Class is it?
- What do you mean?
- Not obvious.

And so on. Good awareness of do's and don'ts lies in the 'and so on'.

This narrative is not loaded with references and the like; far from it. That's not the point. But when I refer you to sources on an aviation website, rather than providing a link that may go dead, I usually follow this format:

home URL>top level topic>sub topic>what you are looking for

In this way, you are more likely to find what I am referring you to.

You can take this guide, written in plain English, directly addressed to you, the drone enthusiast and pilot, buy a drone, and start flying privately, legally and safely. Or you can decide, having read it: 'Now I am going to get licensed'. And, perhaps, next level: 'I am going to fly drones as a professional. And why not set up myself up as an operator?'

Section 1

Let's Talk About Drones

The road map

- In section 1 we'll briefly look at a mixed bag of information, not in detail (that will come later). We'll find out what drones are, what they are called, what the legal framework is in South Africa, and the like. We'll get an idea of the world in which civilian drones operate.
- Section 2 deals with a question that many people ask: how can I fly a drone privately?
- Section 3 tackles the next concern: what does it mean to fly a drone commercially and professionally?
- Section 4 builds on section 3 with the question: how do I become a licensed drone pilot? It describes the Remote Pilot Certificate – the one you want – in detail. It is a comprehensive section.
- Section 5 is about the next step, which is the advanced licence called the Remote Pilot Licence. It is a short section.
- Section 6 explains what an operator is. A pilot may be an operator, that is, own a business certified to fly drones, but an operator is needed to operate drones.
- Section 7 provides an overview of what flying drones entails in our neighbouring countries that have drone legislation. Their situation is quite different from the South African situation.
- Section 8 offers a handy package of documents and forms – not for legal use, just for information. Some of these forms are eye-opening.

Flying drones is part and parcel of aviation. Aviation is heavily regulated. Aviation 'air law' creates swathes of terminology and rules, which are often incomprehensible unless one knows what the drafters actually mean.

My aim, in this guide, is to make it as simple as possible – that is, as simple as the law allows me to reduce it to in plain English and common sense.

So, let's begin with an 'obvious' question:

What are the drone rules called?

Aviation is framed by 'air law'. Drones are no exception.

The expression 'air law' is often misunderstood. It is the umbrella expression used for more than a century now to qualify all rules and regulations that frame civil aviation – from aircraft lights to runway designs to sick bags and what to do if your engine just stops mid-air (you can't park on the side). Pilots have to study for and pass an exam on 'air law'. And to address any sort of confusion, right now: 'aviation law' is something else; it refers to subjects such as air services licensing, aircraft trading, finance and leasing, litigation, airport concessions, and so on. I am not dealing with aviation law in this guide.

For the South African Civil Aviation Authority (SACAA), 'air law' comprises **SA-CARS, which are the Regulations** (the general rules) and **SA-CATS, which are the Technical Standards** (the finer details). Together, they comprise over 2,000 pages. I won't say more about them, except that South Africa is not alone, far from it: the Australian Civil Aviation Safety Authority (CASA) has a very similar schedule. The UK Civil Aviation Authority (CAA), by contrast, is quite different. The European Union Aviation Safety Agency (EASA) and the US Federal Aviation Administration (FAA), the two most developed civil aviation bodies, have comparable but far more complex systems.

If a flyer sticks to 'air law', there is little that an insurance lawyer can do if your drone (actually, 'you') unfortunately causes an accident. If you stick to 'air law', the rules, you should be fine. If you don't follow air law, or any of its rules, you can be in real trouble with the police, with SACAA, and with the law. You don't need to know all 2,000 pages; for drones there are far fewer pages. And you'll find them here, in plain English, giving you a practical understanding of the do's and don'ts, what you need to know, and leaving out what you don't need to know.

All advice or references in this guide are based on current SACAA regulations and standards. Save for one or two occasions, you will be spared legal language, knotty references and technical lingo. But, rest assured, if the tone of this guide is light, the law is doing some heavy lifting in the background.

Drones, all sorts

What's in a word?

Long before the drone, aviation knew of '**pilotless aircraft**', meaning: no pilot on board and at the controls. The term appeared in 1929 in a protocol amending the earlier Paris Convention of 1919 on civil aviation, and it was restated by the 1944 Convention on International Civil Aviation Organization (ICAO) in article 8 (if history interests you) and reads:

Pilotless aircraft

No aircraft capable of being flown without a pilot shall be flown without a pilot over the territory of a contracting State without special authorization by that State and in accordance with the terms of such authorization. Each contracting State undertakes to insure that the flight of such aircraft without a pilot in regions open to civil aircraft shall be so controlled as to obviate danger to civil aircraft.

Don't think this provision is collecting dust. It explains, for example, why you cannot fly your drone less than 10km from an aerodrome (see page 19). And this is just one example among many.

Today we don't say 'pilotless' but 'unmanned', and to quote an EASA official: 'An unmanned aircraft is an aircraft without a pilot on board. Please note that this does not exclude to carry passengers.'

The word **drone** is used in reference to its characteristic noise, similar to that of some insects – the drone fly or rather the bumble bee. The word is an English adaptation of the French word 'bourdon' (the same insect) or 'hommelby' in Afrikaans. The Russian musician Nicolai Rimsky-Korsakov is famous for his stunning musical imitation of a drone, the *Flight of the Bumblebee*. In the 1980s the word 'drone' took over from 'robot' to qualify

aerial drones; basically the usual meaning of 'drone' changed and it began to be used commonly in the early 2000s to refer to that nice little machine you want to fly, legally. That's all there is to it.

For qualifying a robotic flying system of great sophistication, the word 'drone' is really basic. But it is a handy shorthand for all sorts of words that have cropped up in recent years. There are many of them (see below), and this is possibly why the word 'drone' remains by default.

All the words used to refer to a 'drone'

The roll call of words for aerial drones

Here is a list of words and their acronyms that refer to aerial, flying drones. How to make some of these words plural remains a great mystery of aviation lingo, but a drone is a drone. This list is given here simply to make sure we cover everything.

- **UAV** (plural: UAVs or UAVS): **Unmanned Aerial Vehicle(s)**. The Japanese aviation regulator, for instance, prefers a UAV and, plural, UAVs.

- **UAS** (plural: UAS or UAs): **Unmanned Aircraft/Aerial System(s)**. One also finds the use of 'a UA'. In South Africa, UA and UAS are used interchangeably to refer to a single drone. In Spain it is always UAS (singular or plural), according to their Agencia Estatal de Seguridad Aérea. I mention this just in case you want to buy a drone on the Costa Brava in the summer.

- **UA**, then, is used for both the above, to mean one UA.

- **UAS** (plural: UAS or UAs) can also refer to **Uncrewed Aircraft System(s)**. 'Uncrewed' is American military lingo and is also used by the Australian CASA.

- **RPA: Remotely Piloted Aircraft** as well as **RPAS, Remotely Piloted Aircraft System(s)** (RPAS or RPAs). This acronym is used in South Africa, but if you ever fly in Australia, you'll have to mind your language: 'An RPA is a drone that is used for hire or reward, commonly referred to as commercial activities', says CASA, but a 'micro RPA' refers to light recreational or commercial drones. You may also find that RPAS means one RPA. It does not matter.

- SACAA uses **RPA, RPAS, UAS** and **UA**, and provides a definition: 'Unmanned Aircraft Systems' (UAS) *means an unmanned aircraft which is piloted from a remote pilot station, excluding model aircraft and toy aircraft.*' But its Safety Assessment Register has announced that: 'The terms RPA and RPAS were replaced by UA and UAS.' Whether this will stick remains an open question. Again, it does not really matter to you as a drone enthusiast.

Advanced Air Mobility

If acronyms don't faze you, there is **AAM – Advanced Air Mobility** – an expression for aircraft that are highly automated, electrically powered, with vertical take-off (VTOL) ability – in plain English: **air taxis**.

In 2024, Australia, Canada, New Zealand, the UK and the USA formed a network designed for the integration and certification of AAM aircraft, thinking ahead to the development of remotely piloted passenger aircraft. This is the next frontier of civil aviation, and we are talking big 'drones'.

Another word, not often used for aerial machines, is **ROVs (Remotely Operated Vehicles)**. Let us take a quick look at ROVs to round off this roll call of words for drones.

ROVs and non-aerial drones

ROVs include:

- **UGVs** (Unmanned Ground Vehicles), also called **USVs** (Unmanned Surface Vehicles, as long as the surface is the ground)
- sea surface and subsea ROVs: **AUVs** (completely **Autonomous** Underwater Vehicles) and **UUVs** (**Unmanned** Underwater Vehicles)

One can play this game of words forever.

Sea ROVs are becoming popular for recreation and, more seriously, for fishing, which recently led to a court decision **forbidding their use in South African waters**.

Maritime Autonomous Surface Ships

This is another striking development. Following a recent decision by the UN International Maritime Organization, there is now something referred to as **MASS** or **Maritime Autonomous Surface Ships**. The long-winded name refers to autonomous and remotely controlled surface ships. MASS also refers to a single ship ('a MASS'). The matter required urgent attention in view of the growing use of drones in piracy, with all sorts of quaint legal questions: for instance, is a pirate MASS a 'vessel'? No, because, it is argued, a 'vessel' must hoist the flag under which it sails.

MASS drones and underwater drones (called 'vehicles') are already gaining momentum, and with AAM they are also the future of drone innovation, enterprise and big money.

In all of the above, 'autonomous' means no pilot, not on board (hence 'unmanned' or 'uncrewed'), and not at a control station. But in drone magazines 'autonomous' is often used to refer to a drone, aerial or not, controlled from a station.

And now: What do I call my drone?

Back to aerial drones: it is unfortunate that there is not yet a blanket agreement in civil aviation on acronyms for 'drones'. The largest aviation regulatory agency, with a global reach, the EASA, in its *EASA Light website* aimed at non-professionals, speaks simply of 'Drones' – alongside VTOLs (vertical take-off and landing aircraft) – but adds UAS between brackets. It goes to show that the terms used are far from set in stone.

My advice is to stay away from overcomplicated terminology. Use UAS and RPAS if you are a licensed remote pilot flying heavier machines, and when you are in conversation with people in the know, or need to be technical. Otherwise stay with drones, which is shorthand for all those words and machines.

What about 'toy aircraft' and 'model aircraft'?

Toy aircraft

I mention what follows just in case you have an argument with friends about it. You will see that the issue is interesting, but not unusual in aviation regulations.

Granted, a 'light' drone (see page 14) is something of a toy. The current definition is: '"Toy aircraft" means a product falling under the definition of aircraft which is designed or intended for use in play by children'. This is hardly helpful in the age of drones. In South Africa, '"child" means a person under the age of 18 years'.

This is why a new definition has been proposed; it has not yet been adopted but it is useful: 'Toy aircraft means a small, unmanned aircraft other than a model aircraft which is designed or intended for play or recreational aviation purposes, weighing less than 250 grams and capable of maximum speed not exceeding 54 Kmh'.

Regarding weight, a heavy flying toy, a drone in disguise, can cause serious damage or personal injury. However, the age limit is missing from the proposal.

Take the EASA: in the European Union a toy aircraft can be a drone provided it is intended to be **played** with by children **under the age of 14**, and it conforms with safety measures that are obligatory for toys, and it is designed for children under the age of 14, which the manufacturer must make specifically clear, and (here comes the crunch) it excludes any product with a combustion engine and/or 'with a sensor able to capture personal data', as the United Kingdom CAA emphasises in line with the British Toy (Safety) regulations.

So legally, for now, a 'child' of 17 can fly a drone, and the family lawyer can argue that it is a toy aircraft used to 'play' (see the definition), if there is an accident that causes damage or injury. Clearly there is a gap in the proposed new definition.

Model aircraft

In South Africa, 'aeromodelling' as it is properly called, falls under a specific part of the Civil Aviation Regulations, 'Aviation Recreation' (SA-CARS Part 149). It is hugely popular and is supervised by a dedicated body, the South African Model Aircraft Association (SAMAA), which is a hundred years old and has some 1,800 members and 81 clubs.

At face value, some drones referred to at pages 14–16 may well fall within the proposed definition of a 'toy aircraft', in terms of their weight. But the proposal about toy aircraft avoids using the word 'private' and prefers 'recreational', a formulation used by the Regulations that deal with model aircraft. Another tangle.

The definition of a model aircraft is at present:

> A non-human-carrying aircraft capable of sustained flight in the atmosphere and used exclusively for air display, recreational use, sport or competitions, operated at approved SAMAA airfields only.

In short, all guidelines and operations are set by SAMAA, and each aero modelling club more or less sets its own rules for operations at their aerodromes. This is a great opportunity for private drone flyers (see page 27).

Next problem: How do you differentiate a light drone from a model aircraft, except that your drone does not look like a Spitfire (although it could)?

The Australians have made a decent effort to make the distinction:

> A model aircraft means any aircraft, other than a balloon or kite, that cannot carry a person, and weighs no more than 150 kg and is used for sport or recreation; or weighs no more than 7 kg and is operated by schools and higher education providers in connection with educational, training and research purposes. It includes drones, along with what are traditionally considered to be model aircraft such as radio-controlled models. The term model aircraft is used to differentiate drones and radio-controlled models used for sport or recreation from drones used for commercial or commercial-like purposes, known as remotely piloted aircraft (RPA).

In short, you have a light drone (see page 14), and you want to fly it for pylon racing, display, aerobatics, and the like, which you are not allowed to do privately (see page 19). You then contact SAMAA (www.samaa.org.za) and ask them where the nearest SAMAA aero modelling club is and if they can accommodate you. Why? Because, as you will read in section 2, you cannot do all that fancy flying with a drone, but at a SAMAA airfield you may well be able to, whether your drone is an aeroplane, a helicopter or a multi-rotor (on these differences, see page 48). But remember that there is a restriction placed on how high you can fly: 'No model aircraft shall be flown higher than 150 feet above the surface', says SACAA.

The final words on drones

To wrap up this general overview, let us focus on the key words 'systems', 'piloted' and 'aircraft'. And let us see what we gain from it.

First, what are 'system(s)'?

To quote the EASA: 'The Regulations use the term UAS, unmanned aircraft system, to refer to a drone, its system and all the other equipment used to control and operate it, such as the command unit, the possible catapult to launch it and others.' In short, **a drone/UAS is an aircraft plus a system**.

The 'system' consists of the command and control link and the control station which, to state the obvious, is not onboard, but controls the actuators that, on the machine, move or prompt the flying components – as well as the fitted sensors (camera, GPS) and the software. That entire 'system' makes the 'remote' part of it possible, while you stand 400ft below your drone.

This is why highly technical literature calls a drone a 'cyber-physical' system.

The implication is that a drone pilot must be able to understand and to handle both an aircraft and a system. The system can be simple or sophisticated.

Second, what does 'piloted' mean?

The EASA again provides an explanation, while slightly complicating the use of RPAS and UAS. But never mind, because this illustrates one key take-away, 'pilot': 'RPAS (Remotely Piloted Aircraft Systems) is a subcategory of UAS, which includes both RPAS and fully autonomous UAS. Fully autonomous UAS fly completely by themselves without the need for any pilot intervention.' The word 'pilot' is the take-away.

There is more here than meets the eye: using the words **'pilot'** and **'piloted'** implies that **training and licensing are required**, because the word 'pilot' in aviation is not used lightly: a pilot carries a licence and obtaining a licence is highly regulated, as detailed in sections 4 and 5.

Third, what does 'aircraft' mean?

The third key take-away is the word 'aircraft'.

The moment 'aircraft' is applied, the whole thing, except for the military, falls under the umbrella of the International Civil Aviation Organization (ICAO). ICAO defines all things in civil aviation, from airport design to sick bags, as already mentioned, but it is guided by **two key principles: safety and uniformity in aviation**. That is, across countries, the same rules and standards, as far as possible, must apply to prevent accidents.

When, later on, we move on to the nitty-gritty of 'drone pilot' licensing or the technical classification of 'drones', the demand for secure standards in order to ensure people's safety will become clear. Unfortunately, uniformity in drone flying, outside the large EASA and FAA domains, has not yet seen the light of day across in most countries. See section 7 on how our neighbouring countries handle drones. But once the word 'aircraft' is mentioned, everything falls into 'aviation', particularly how to define each component, each phase, each action engaged in flying a drone, and getting licensed.

Now, let us look at how you can fly a drone privately.

Section 2

I Fly My Drone Privately

Some say they fly their drones for 'fun', but 'fun' is not a legal term. In aviation we say 'privately'. Be careful with the word 'recreation' because of the overlap between model aircraft flying ('aeromodelling') (see page 10) and drones.

What does 'private' mean?

This is what SACAA says: *Private operation* – means the use of an UAS for an individual's personal and private purposes where there is no commercial outcome, interest or gain.

Scenario: you fly a drone (that is, the sort of drone you'll find described on page 14) at a braai, on your property, or at a friend's house, because he asked you, 'please can you film it?' (He must give you permission; he is a friend, but keep his WhatsApp for the record in case of an accident.) You get nice footage, and you use it to advertise your catering business. Then it is not private, and what you are doing is illegal. Just be careful. On a small scale, it will probably go unnoticed, but if someone discovers that they are in an advert, and they get upset, this could lead to serious trouble.

What type of drone can fly privately and who can fly it?

There is no minimum (or maximum) age requirement

That is why, basically, you are not entitled to call yourself a remote private 'pilot'. Licensed pilots have minimum as well as maximum age requirements. You are just handling a light drone. A youngster can, and an elderly person can.

Any age is fine, as long as the rules are observed by your 15-year-old.

Specifically, only two types of drones are allowed to be flown privately. In aviation, the word is 'Classes' not 'types' (types are something else). But you can say type if you prefer …

You can fly only two 'Classes' of drones privately.

They are called RPAS in SACAA's list (and UAS as well).

We are going to differentiate those two Classes of light drones from Classes of heavier drones used for commercial operations (see section 3).

CLASS	TABLE 1: RPAS CLASSIFICATION			
	Line-of-Sight	Energy (kJ)	Height (ft)	MTOM (kg)
Class 1A	R-VLOS/VLOS	E < 15	h < 400	m < 1.5
Class 1B	R-VLOS/VLOS/EVLOS	E < 15	h < 400	m < 7

The drones you can fly 'privately' are called 'Classes 1A and 1B of RPAS'. SACAA says: 'Private operation of UAS shall be conducted only in R-VLOS with a Class 1A or 1B UAS.'

What are Classes?

Classes are determined by energy on impact, the height at which your drone is allowed to fly, and its weight (or 'mass', as in maximum take-off mass (MTOM)).

So, you can go to a shop, or shop online, pick a drone, and check the specs. Some sellers will be specific, some not, and usually they do an overkill with the camera specs, which is not what you want to make sure that the drone you are buying fits the 'private' use of it. You must check the MTOM, or the 'weight'.

About weight, MTOM, pounds and kilos

A package will indicate the weight, not the MTOM. So you buy a drone with a 'weight' as it says on the box of 1.4kg, you do some fiddling 'modif', and you add a nice camera: you have now changed the MTOM, and you are probably above the legal limit. In manned aviation, fuel is included in the MTOM. This is unlikely with a light drone. The result? You add weight, you exceed the limit, and you cannot fly your drone.

But if you are unhappy with the weight limit and you want a heavier machine, above 7kg, then you cannot fly privately. You'll have to go commercial (see sections 3 and 4).

You can fly only below 400ft (roughly 122m, not 150m as you will read on some websites).

Beware of buying drones manufactured for the American market that may be rated in pounds (and even ounces) only and not kilograms (or grams). We use kg and g.

Energy and risk

Don't worry about the energy or kinetic impact energy as private use is graded <15 kJ and this would take a long explanation with lots of physics – not the intention here.

The idea is that a 200g drone that is out of power or is getting out of control that falls from 100ft is less likely to kill someone than one of 6kg falling from 400ft. Some years back, scientific studies were done on the kinetic impact of light drones on human beings, especially the frequency of head injuries, and the results were so worrying that the rules were tightened.

Now it is time to launch that shiny quad … BUT you can't, because all sorts of rules kick in. Look at the warning on the box.

The warning on the box

The box will have a small print warning which says something like: **'The user of this drone must observe rules set by Civil Aviation'.**

No drone can be sold without an advisory notice which 'notifies' (a legal obligation) the buyer of the existence of rules that must be obeyed in the country where the drone is flown. The manufacturer need not give you the rules, or even tell you where to find them. Sometimes the manufacturer will refer you to a Civil Aviation website, not necessarily SACAA! You are supposed to know the law. If you have the time, you can read the legislation online. It runs into hundreds of pages. **Or you can continue reading this book.**

Let us now look at this slate of rules. You are standing in your garden, ready to fly your drone over the braai, but on second thoughts you decide you'd better read the next few pages. Hopefully, there will still be chops and boerewors left when you've finished reading this section.

The basic rules

Overarching rule

The law says:

'It is the full responsibility of the remote pilot of the UAS to fly his/her aircraft safely and not endanger [the] safety of another aircraft, any person or property.'

In other words: 'A remote pilot must observe all statutory requirements relating to liability, privacy and any other laws enforceable by any other authorities.'

The Class and visual line-of-sight rule

Only fly a drone of Class **1A or 1B** and only in **R-VLOS**.

R stands for restricted, VLOS stands for visual line-of-sight. Don't worry about the other mentions of VLOS, E-VLOS noted in the list (see page 14). What matters to you as a private user is R-VLOS.

The restrictions are tough, as we are going to see. But there is good news too: you can fly your Class 1A or 1B **day and night** – as long as you stick to the R-VLOS rules (to quote: 'A UA may not be operated at night except— (*a*) in R-VLOS operation').

What do R and VLOS actually mean?

This means that you must always keep your drone in sight: it is the VLOS or **visual line-of-sight** rule but within **restricted conditions**, the R. It does not mean that provided you can see the drone you are free to let it fly. No, R implies restricted conditions, as described below.

Visual contact at all times

This sounds easy but constant visual contact makes all sorts of demands.

You **cannot look away at any time**; the law says that you must '**maintain visual contact**'.

You must **keep 'visual contact' with the naked eye**: you cannot use binoculars, goggles, smart phones, vision enhancers, and so on.

You can wear your **prescription glasses** or **corrective lenses**; in fact, you should, as without them you are unlikely to have the drone in sight at all times. A basic precaution in aviation (called 'redundancy') is to have a spare pair of spectacles: if you drop your glasses, and you have no spare pair, then you are illegal.

You cannot have someone standing next to you doing the looking while you control the drone (no 'observer'). You cannot ask someone to look at the drone for you while you are looking for the glasses you've dropped or fiddling with something.

There must be no obstruction (building, mast, bridge, pylon) that prevents you from **seeing your drone at all times**.

You must fly in 'clear weather': there must be no low cloud, mist, fog, rain, haze, dust or smoke preventing you from seeing your drone at all times. If you are near the coast, you know how **fog** can come up all of a sudden (and not only in George). The same applies if you live in a valley. Lesson: anticipate what can happen.

You can fly your drone at night, in clear weather (no cloud, no mist, no haze, no dust, no smoke, no rain – as above) BUT remember that **it can take up to 10 minutes for your eyes to transition from daylight to night**, so do what aviation pilots do: put on sunglasses as the sun is setting and don't look directly at it until it has fallen behind the horizon. Also, get yourself a frontal night light that you can switch to red mode if needed (you don't want to blind a fellow 'dronie' in the vicinity). It may sound like overkill for a fun drone that is flying for 22 minutes, but things do happen.

No First Person View (FPV) drones

FPV drones fly low, fly fast, fly for short periods, fly 'immersive' and **use goggles**. You cannot fly 1A and 1B privately because of the use of goggles (analogue or digital). Besides, FPV drones frequently crash, and are used for racing or aerobatic-like moves that are not allowed in privately flying drones. You will not find it spelt out in the rules (yet), but **general rules apply** and it follows that **FPV drone flying is not acceptable**.

However, FPV drones are a niche area for highly skilled enthusiasts, who are in growing demand by the film industry in particular. But, once one mentions the word 'industry', then it falls into 'commercial' flying (see section 3). So, if you want to explore FPV drones, your best route is to discuss it with a flight school that specialises in drones (see page 46) or to get in touch with a certified operator (section 6). You can also contact SAMAA (model aircraft, see page 10).

The altitude restrictions

(1) Your drone is allowed **to fly up to below 400ft**: that is the vertical distance, height or altitude (never mind the word). Altitude is NEVER in metres, always in feet (ft). It is calculated from where you stand, hence Above Ground Level (AGL). If you stand on a beach, at sea level, you've got 400ft above you to fly your drone. If you stand on top of the *Ribbokkop* in the Golden Gates, at some 9,000ft, you still have 400ft above you to fly (except that it is a South African National Park, and a no-fly zone – see page 24). In the case of a building, 400ft is about 40 stories, including the ground floor.

(2) Your drone must stay **below the height of the highest building within 300m** of the drone (not of you: of the *drone*) (see the picture on page 22).

The lateral distance restriction

Your drone cannot be more than **500m distance** from you: this is the radius or 'lateral' distance from where you stand. By visual comparison, and taking an average house plot with a frontage of 30m, 500m represents a fairly long street with some 16 houses.

The not near a 'manned' aircraft rule

Manned aircraft include aeroplanes, helicopters, manned 'free' and captive balloons and what are called 'non type-certificated aircraft' (paragliders, paratrikes, gyroplanes, hang-gliders, microlight aeroplanes, parachutes). It is unclear if an unmanned free or captive balloon or even a line-controlled kite are included, but the basic rule is: if in doubt, don't fly near to it. 'Near' is not easy to assess because of the speed of your drone and the speed of a powered aircraft. Use your common sense.

This rule also applies to keeping away from other drones. **No swarm or formation flying**. And **no aerobatics**.

The wind risk factor

The wind can play tricks and send your drone on a collision course. Always check the wind, which comes with two factors: the **surface wind velocity** (speed) ('surface' because you are below 1,500ft, usually considered to be the limit) AND **wind gusts**. Go to the website windy.com and check the details for the time of your fun flight. Small drones are light. It goes without saying that a gust of wind will lead to a loss of control.

The keep 10km away from aerodromes rule – but where are they?

Your **drone must not enter a 10km radius of an aerodrome**, airport, helipad, helistop or airfield. Without getting technical about what the reference point is from which it is calculated, just keep your drone 10km away from the fence or boundary.

For fun: If you cross-reference the 10km rule with the 500m radius rule, it means that you can stand 10,500m from OR Tambo fence, and be legit. Just.

How to find out about aerodromes

At the time of writing, there are some 368 registered aerodromes and airfields, and 68 airports, including ten international ones.

So, if you plan to fly your drone at a camp site and you don't know the lay of the land, it is better to make sure there is no 'hidden' airfield nearby. It is best to ask a police station or the nearest aeroclub. But you can also check the SACAA website (www.caa.co.za and follow: Industry>Aeronautical Information> Aeronautical Information Publication (AIP)>Aerodromes). It is regularly updated.

The keep 50m away from people/buildings rule

Fly 50m away from

Any person or group of persons (like sport fields, road races, stadiums, schools, social events, open air churches, beaches with a group of frolickers, etc)

Any structure or building

Any public road: this also means that you cannot take-off or land your drone on a public road, and you cannot fly along it, playing 'runway here I come'.

Please **beware of power lines and zip lines**. You will not find this warning in the rules, but experienced pilots will tell you that they are a real hazard, often hard to see and quite low.

The not over another property rule

Do not fly over any property without permission from the property or landowner (not the tenant, but the owner, and get permission in writing or record it on your smartphone).

The not next to or above State locations rule

Do not fly near nuclear power plants, prisons, police stations, crime scenes, courts of law, national key points or strategic installations (power stations and pylons, large national dams).

And the Don't be Daft rules

The no drop rule

Do not release, dispense, drop, deliver or deploy any object or substance from your drone.

I was told an anecdote about a local fisherman who, privately, uses a drone to drop bait. Whether it is kaapse humour or not, it is forbidden.

The don't carry anything dangerous rule

The no drag or tow rule

Your drone should not drag small banners, eg 'I LuV My Drone', or tow (!) another drone.

Picture to illustrate distances to respect R-VLOS rules

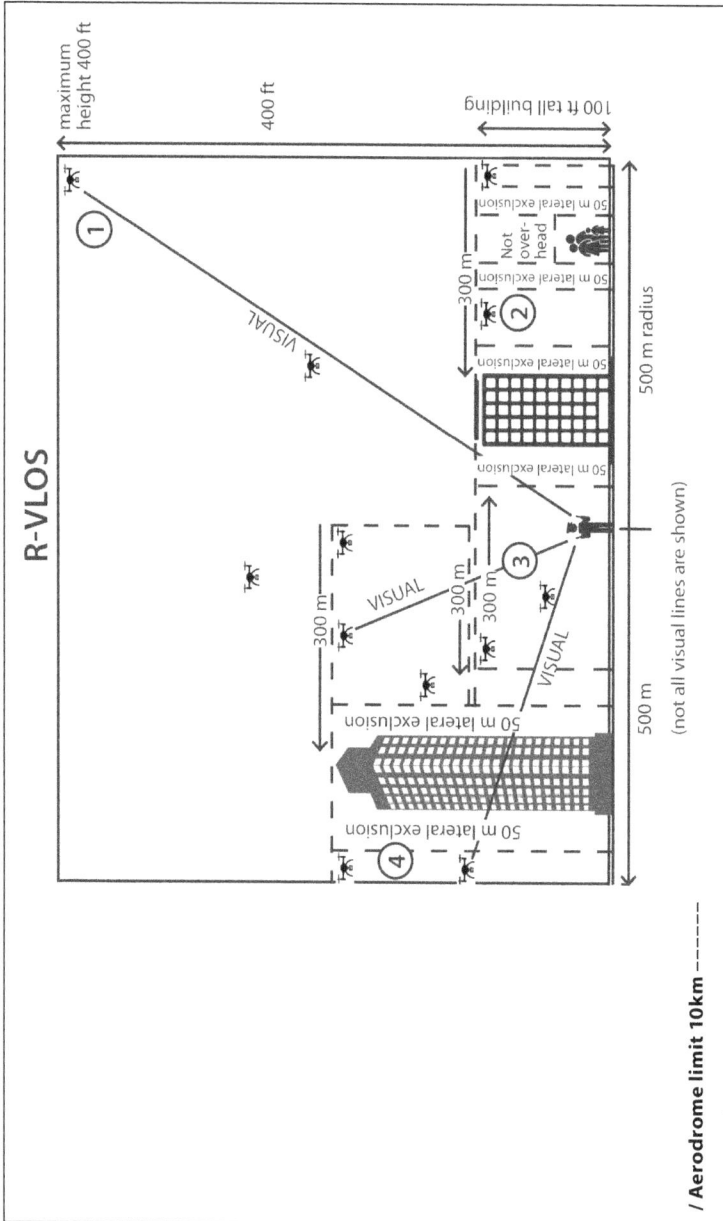

R-VLOS

maximum height 400 ft

400 ft

100 ft tall building

50 m lateral exclusion

50 m lateral exclusion

50 m lateral exclusion

50 m lateral exclusion

50 m lateral exclusion

50 m lateral exclusion

Not over-head

300 m

300 m

300 m

300 m

300 m

VISUAL

VISUAL

VISUAL

500 m radius

500 m

(not all visual lines are shown)

/ Aerodrome limit 10km ------

The circled numbers in the picture refer to four situations.

In all situations, unobstructed, unaided and visual contact with the drone must be maintained.

Situation 1: The drone flies up to the maximum vertical limit of 400ft above the ground where you stand and at a maximum horizontal limit of 500m from you (called the radius).

Situation 2: The drone must, laterally, be 50m or more from a person, a building, an official facility, an assembly, a road, etc, and it cannot fly along, take off from or land on a road (not shown) – nor can it be directly overhead people (as shown).

Situation 3: In this scenario, the tallest building within 300m from your drone is 100ft high (which equals, roughly, 10 floors, ground floor included). Your drone must then fly below the height of the building, that is below 100ft. So, don't hover over the top floor penthouse to get a nice view of sunbathers.

A 'building' can be any sort of structure.

Be aware that the drone cannot get closer than 50m from the building, and it cannot be further then 500m from you.

Situation 4: Here you are at risk of losing visual line-of-sight if your drone flies around the corner of the skyscraper. You must always **maintain visual contact.**

Note the 10km radius from an aerodrome **to the drone** being itself positioned at a maximum of 500m from you.

And now, within those parameters, the rules are mostly related to the airspace where you would like to fly your drone.

Some special airspace rules

In case you are not fully aware of it, most airplanes and choppers you see flying around do so mostly, especially near cities, in one or several airspaces. Each category of airspace has a defined radius, a specific vertical dimension, and pilots obey or rely on air traffic services. The purpose of various airspaces is to prevent collisions by ensuring 'separation', and helping traffic, in broad terms.

How does this impact the private flying of drones? Not much, because **you are flying privately in 'uncontrolled airspace'**, that is: no 'tower' with air traffic controllers is telling you what to do, and you are not asking them for information. In fact, how can they radio you, or you contact them, while you fly your drone over that braai, and what for in the first place? To exchange recipes?

Note that there are airspaces that may be a concern to you as a private drone flyer. When flying a drone Class 1A or 1B privately, you need not know what they are, or why they are in place, or how to operate within them in detail, but you do need to be aware of some of them, as explained below.

Not in controlled/dangerous/restricted/prohibited airspace rule

If you want to do some private flying with a drone Class 1A or 1B in an area that is unfamiliar, take note of the following:

- **Paragliding airspace** is a danger zone. If you want to fly your drone there, you must ask for prior authorisation. The risk is serious.

- **No entry zones** exist where any flying from the ground up is forbidden. For example, Firgrove near Gordon's Bay, Western Cape, is a prohibited airspace: no aircraft or drones whatsoever. They'll shoot your drone down.

An excellent online site provides maps of such zones, plus a host of information: https://drones.org.za/dronemap2/map.html

If in doubt, check with SACAA (0860 267 435, well in advance) or just go to your nearest flight school or aeroclub and ask. Pilots help each other and you will be shown a chart, or aeronautical map, of the area you are interested in.

Not in National Parks rule except with commercial authorisation

Private drone flying is forbidden

The general aviation rule is no flying below 2,500 ft above the highest point of any national park. **Since you can only fly <400 ft, you can't fly there; it's logical.**

In addition to the National Parks there are also some 28 'Vulture Colonies and Restaurants'; while it is unlikely you will camp out at their bespoke feeding grounds and nests, who knows? The best way to make sure is to call SACAA and ask.

Fines for infringement are hefty. You'll be arrested.

Commercial purposes, such as filming/photography

If you want to use your drone for a **commercial purpose** such as filming, all SACAA rules regarding commercial flying apply (section 3) as well as the need for a licensed operator (section 6), and permission must be obtained from the South African National Parks administration. And, of course, the pilot must be licensed (section 4). The application is detailed: check the first two pages provided on page 103, for information only. It gives you a fair idea. You can download it here: https://www.sanparks.org/wp-content/uploads/2021/05/app_form_drones.pdf

Private game parks?

It is up to the owner to grant you explicit permission; if they do, be careful with a private game park abutting a National Park, as there is a risk of incursion. People have been arrested.

The good news

There are a number of things that you do NOT NEED to do, believe it or not, as a private handler of a drone – just in case someone mentions them to you and starts arguing about it:

- **Time of flight** need not be recorded but it is a good idea to time your joy ride, one way or another, if you want to move on to commercial drone flying. In aviation we use Co-ordinated Universal Time (UTC), and not local time. In South Africa our local time is called SAST, which is two hours ahead of UTC, or UTC+02:00. UTC is also called Zulu time and prefixed Z, a standard used in civilian aviation (so that all flight plans, traffic, etc can be coordinated). Local time is prefixed B, for Bravo. But only do it to get into the habit of it, if you think you'll move on to a 'commercial' licence. I have mentioned wind and clear air conditions: when you check them on whatever reliable meteorological site you are using, make sure it is in local time and not in UTC. Lots can happen to the weather in that two hours differential.

- You do not need to keep a drone logbook (a 'flight folio' record, flight by flight of the drone's flight and performance). But why not do so anyway? There is no need to use a professional one (that is part of your training and legal obligation as a licensed pilot – section 4): a simple school notebook will do. You jot down the date of flight, the drone make and model (especially if you fly more than one), the location of your flight, the total flight time and any issue or interesting feature.

- You do not have to keep your own **pilot logbook**; that is really for licensed pilots. A logbook is an aviation pilot's most prized (and legally compliant) possession. If you ever make the move to being licensed that personal record (which has no legal value) could show that you are not a newcomer. Again: it will have no legal value.

- You do not need a **power reserve** (electric charge or fuel of at least 10% of charge necessary to complete a flight). However, you must have enough charge or fuel to complete the flight as intended, which falls under the rule of being 'responsible' and avoiding risk.

- You do not need a **first aid kit**. But who knows? It may be useful.

- You do not need a hand-held **fire extinguisher**. But it can't do any harm.

The welcoming aeromodelling aerodromes

As mentioned earlier, numerous SAMAA-affiliated aerodromes (such as Barnstormers Kempton Park) usually welcome drone flyers. The 10km distance rule falls away but you have to comply with the rules of each particular aero modelling club.

In fact, if you are a private drone enthusiast, flying at SAMAA airfields is possibly your best choice. You'll learn a great deal about collision avoidance and general handling. But do not forget that 'no model aircraft shall be flown higher than 150 ft above the surface', unless SACAA has given permission otherwise.

So far, there is one element of the equation that we have not looked at: You, the 'humanware'. And a simple question: are you fit to fly?

Are you fit to fly?

In aviation, this refers to Human Factors. Being 'fit to fly' falls under the overarching SACAA rule: 'It is the full responsibility of the remote pilot of the UAS to fly his/her aircraft safely and **not endanger** [the] safety of another aircraft, any person or property.'

What does this mean?

To be responsible, you must be medically fit to fly a drone

Fortunately you don't need a licence to fly a Class 1A or 1B privately. There is no minimum or maximum age requirement; you don't need to be registered, so you don't need a 'medical' – an examination by a certified aviation doctor (see page 50).

But there are basic rules that will keep you out of trouble if you cause a serious accident and if an insurer asks how 'responsible' you were flying your drone over that braai, and causing serious trauma to one of your guests. Or just for your own sake.

The I'M SAFE checklist

In aviation there is a quick way of making sure that a pilot is fit to fly: **I'M SAFE**.

I'M SAFE stands for a list of questions about one's fitness on the day of a flight, any flight. Your Class 1A or 1B is an aircraft. So, before you pack and go to film (privately) your sister's wedding at a wine farm (with permission) run through these items quickly. It takes one minute. If you reply 'Yes' to any of these questions, rather leave the drone at home.

I – do I feel Ill?

M – did I take any **M**edication that can making me lose focus? (flu medications are the worst)

S – am I **S**tressed, do I lack **S**leep?

A – did I drink **A**lcohol recently? (in strict aviation rules, a pilot should not drink 8 hrs before a flight more than 0,02gr/100ml, roughly a double whiskey and a large glass of wine).

F – am I **F**atigued? That is, not really feeling up to it (in strict aviation rules, it is far tougher). Don't let anyone pressurise you to 'please get your drone!'

E – have I **E**aten something that upset me? Am I starving? You don't want to get sick while handling your drone, or be distracted by wanting a quick bite.

All these rules are far tougher in manned or commercial aviation, but they are common-sense guidelines for the private drone user. A 'light' drone can cause heavy injuries.

The next step in the world of flying drones is to go 'commercial' and get licensed.

Section 3

What is Flying 'Commercially'?

Why would you want to fly 'commercially?'

Flying drones as a business venture is getting bigger and bigger by the day, both worldwide and locally. South Africa is a prime location in many respects: natural resources, mineral wealth, agriculture, conservation, the need for the increased and reliable surveillance of industrial and property sites, to name just a few.

The commercial uses of drones and the business and employment opportunities are obvious. The global market is projected to reach some US$3 billion by 2029.

Drones are becoming key instruments in industrial site surveillance, property marketing, film and photography, agricultural activities, emergency services, land surveying and mapping, mining and, of course, conservation. The last items explain why neighbouring countries rich in wildlife and minerals (Namibia, Zimbabwe and Botswana) have such restrictive laws (see section 7), not to mention our own restrictions placed on the film industry leveraging the gorgeous resources of our vast and unique national parks. Our own restrictions also prevent foreign pilots and entities having a free rein in the areas of development mentioned. There are golden commercial opportunities, which means getting licensed as a pilot and/or an operator (see sections 4 and 6). Staying 'private' will not suffice.

Clearly, the key word is 'commercial'. There is a lot of confusion about the word 'commercial' and what it entails. This is not clearly explained on many websites.

What is 'commercial' drone flying ?

In terms of the law it means flying a drone for a commercial outcome, interest or gain. But this needs to be further unpacked.

Flying drones 'commercially' covers three factors:

- the drone itself being legally fit for the operation of commercial flying
- the commercial operation of flying a drone
- the act, as a pilot, of legally flying a drone that is fit for a commercial operation and is part of a commercial operation, which means being licensed

All the above are usually grouped together under 'commercial'.

Step by step

First, there is your drone

This is the easy part. Is the drone classified as a drone fit for a commercial operation? **Drones Class 1A and 1B are for 'private use'.**

Second, there is the operator

This is whoever pays you, rewards you, or compensates you for flying a drone for which the operator is a SACAA-certified operator. See section 6 for the details.

The operator who employs you, the pilot, can have three different legal statuses:

- **a commercial entity**, that is, a business which employs you, as a pilot, to fly a drone in order for that business to perform a service for its client
- **a corporate entity**, that is, an entity (usually a business) which employs you to fly a drone in order for that business to perform a service for itself (eg a mine employs a pilot to do its own surveillance)
- **a non-profit entity**, such as a university lab which has a drone for some research, and employs you, as a pilot, to fly it.

Why is this hair-splitting important?

Because these entities and only these entities can employ you or reward you or compensate you for flying 'commercially'. All three, when they employ pilots to fly drones, **must be registered as 'operators', and only operators can make you perform a 'commercial' flight** (see section 6). You can of course set up your own business, register as an operator, and act as pilot.

Whether your employer as an operator is or is not a 'commercial' enterprise, and is a corporate or a non-profit, does not make any difference to you as a pilot who flies for that entity, and gets paid one way or another: **your action as a pilot is commercial anyway**.

Advice to pilots: If an entity, commercial, corporate or non-profit, approaches you to fly for them, make sure that they are certified operators. If they are not, it is illegal.

Operator: This word leads to lot of confusion for those who are not already in the know about all things aviation. Yes, pilots 'operate' aircraft, but they are not 'operators'. In aviation, the operator is the SACAA-certified entity that is responsible for performing a number of legal and managerial tasks to ensure the safety and legality of aviation operations, from registration to safety drills (the list of duties is extensive).

Operations: Unfortunately, and this creates confusion, SA-CARS (regulations) refer to 'Operating Flight Rules' and SA-CATS (technical standards) refer to 'Flight Operations', including 'UAS Operations', which is a detailed list of what you, as a pilot flying your drone, can do ('privileges') and cannot do ('limitations') (eg land on a public road). In short, these are the actual 'operations' of flying. But you do them as a pilot, not as an operator. One day someone will hopefully sort out the language, which dates back to the early ages of modern aviation.

Third, there is you, the pilot

Do you want to fly in order to make money, regardless of whether the certified operator who holds the registration of the drone is a commercial venture, a corporate or a non-profit? If the answer is 'yes', **you need a licence** called an RPC or an RPL (see sections 4 and 5).

Unfortunately, there is no document called a 'commercial licence' for remote pilots. In manned aviation there is indeed a Commercial Pilot Licence, but not for someone flying drones 'commercially', to make money.

What does it mean 'to make money'? It is defined, to reiterate the point, as flying for 'a commercial outcome, an interest or gain'. If you fly a drone and are paid for it, or have a quantifiable or profitable interest in doing it, or gain some compensation or gift, then as a pilot your action is 'commercial'. But remember: the drone you are flying must not be Class 1A or 1B.

Private, commercial, corporate – still unclear?

Let's look at two scenarios.

Scenario 1: Private, commercial, corporate?

You own a registered farm and you want to do some overflying (mapping, photos, surveillance), but you realise that you need a bigger drone that falls outside the 'private' 1A and 1B Classes, and flies in restricted conditions R-VLOS. If you were to go ahead, it would be a corporate operation because it would be 'in aid' of your own farming activities.

BUT to fly a heavier drone, the kind legally accepted for non-private use (see below), you would need to buy one, register it, and apply to be an operator (see section 6).

You can't turn around and say: but I have a licence, an RPC (see section 4)! Sure you do, but you have to be an operator, even for a 'corporate operation', whether *you* fly that drone or whether you employ a licensed pilot to do it. Operators are discussed in section 6. That is the route if you don't want to contract an outsider, an operator who will do the job for you, in which case the operation is out of your hands.

Now if, on your farm, you are happy to use your 'private' drones to do basic photography or surveillance, and the restrictions R-VLOS placed on 'private' flying are not a bother (the main restriction is distance, but see page 22 for details), then you can do so. For any non-1A and 1B Class drones, operator status (registration of the drone and certification of the operator) kicks in. Otherwise, you can contract a drone company to do the job and then it is out of your hands. For the licensed remote pilot, whether employed by you or by an outside entity, it remains a commercial act.

Scenario 2: Private or commercial?

You hold a licence, an RPC, but you own a drone that is fit for private use as per the specs (Class 1A and 1B drone), to be flown in R-VLOS (basically around the pumpkin patch). You film (again!) your sister's (second) wedding. Your flying is private and personal. Now, you sell the lovely footage, or you monetise it on a social platform, or you decide to use it to advertise your new business. What happens?

It is now commercial (gain, profit, reward, money) and illegal: to begin with, a 1A and 1B drone cannot be flown for a pilot's commercial acts. You insist: but I've got an RPC! Fine, but it does not apply here because a drone 1A and 1B is flown privately. And, by the way, who is the operator? It can get even more confusing than that.

Bottom line: don't try to cross over. Fly private, or fly licensed, with the correct drone.

Now, what drones are legal for a 'commercial' flight?

What drones are legal for 'commercial' flying?

Before we look at them, here is a reminder of SACAA's 'Classification of UAS/UA' or 'RPAS Classification' (same thing, different wording):

Class	Table 1: RPAS classification			
	Line-of-Sight	**Energy (kJ)**	**Height (ft)**	**MTOM (kg)**
Class 1A	R-VLOS/VLOS	E < 15	h < 400	m < 1.5
Class 1B	R-VLOS/VLOS/EVLOS	E < 15	h < 400	m < 7
Class 1C	VLOS/EVLOS	E < 34	h < 400	m < 20
Class 2A	VLOS/EVLOS	E > 34	h < 400	m < 20
Class 2B	**Experimental / Research**			
Class 3A	BVLOS	E > 34	h < 400	m < 150
Class 3B	VLOS/EVLOS	Any	h > 400	m < 150
Class 4A	BVLOS	Any	h > 400	m < 150
Class 4B	Any	Any	Any	m > 150
Class 5	Reserved	Reserved	Reserved	Reserved

Reserved – means to be defined in the future

h – means height above the surface

E – means energy at impact

Note: All operations are limited to radio line-of-sight

Classes of drones that are of interest to you commercially fall into two bands, in addition to Classes 1A and 1B already dealt with.

Classes 1C and 2A: 20kg maximum weight

Classes 1C and 2A are allowed to **fly up to 400ft** (always AGL, above the ground where you stand), and have a 'weight' or MTOM **up to 20kg**. Impact energy is either below or above 34kJ, and that is, as mentioned, basically linked to velocity and impact – plain English: damage caused.

Class 1C	VLOS/EVLOS	E < 34	h < 400	m < 20
Class 2A	VLOS/EVLOS	E > 34	h < 400	m < 20

In this band, Classes 1C and 2A, the drone can be flown in **visual line-of-sight** or in **extended visual line-of-sight**. This is explained in the next section. See the picture on page 38.

Classes 3 and 4: < or > 150kg weight

In **Classes 3 and 4**, while the height of **400ft varies**, the 'weight' allowed can go **up to and above 150kg**. These are hefty machines.

Class 3A	BVLOS	E > 34	h < 400	m < 150
Class 3B	VLOS/EVLOS	Any	h > 400	m < 150
Class 4A	BVLOS	Any	h > 400	m < 150
Class 4B	Any	Any	Any	m > 150

In this band, Classes 3 and 4, the drones are heavier and may be flown **B-VLOS** on top of **V-LOS** and **E-VLOS**. This is explained in the next section. See the picture on page 41.

Lines-of-sight for flying a drone commercially

So far we have dealt with the technical specs of the drone. Now, let us look at the flying restrictions in terms of how far and how high you can fly your drone 'commercially'.

In South Africa drones are flown in RLOS, 'a direct electronic point-to-point contact between a transmitter and receiver'. 'R' stands for 'radio'. You are on the ground, your drone is up there, and a radio line is cast in-between – with apologies to technically savvy readers if this sounds trite but that's the basic idea.

RLOS is 'subdivided' into:

R-VLOS: restricted visual line-of-sight

VLOS: visual line-of-sight

E-VLOS: extended visual line-of-sight

B-VLOS: beyond visual line-of-sight

VLOS, E-VLOS and B-VLOS are integrated or added to your licence. VLOS is the standard rating for a remote pilot licence or RPC (see section 4 about the RPC). E-VLOS and B-VLOS are additional ratings.

It is mentioned here to avoid confusion about what is a line-of-sight (how 'far' each type of drone is classified in terms of flying: 3A and 4A are only B-VLOS) and what your legal right is, as per your licence (RPC or RPL), to fly with a given line-of-sight (on RPC and RPL see sections 4 and 5). If you hold an RPC rated E-VLOS, you cannot fly B-VLOS.

A reminder: Fly private, fly R-VLOS

A private pilot flying 1A and 1B drones can fly only in R-VLOS, as we have seen in section 2.

Fly commercial, fly VLOS, E-VLOS, B-VLOS or R-VLOS

A licensed pilot is **not restricted** in terms of line-of-sight, as is a private dronie. A 'commercial' RPC or RPL licensed pilot (sections 4 and 5) can fly a drone with three categories of line-of-sight: VLOS, E-VLOS and/or B-VLOS.

What the *drone* is allowed to do is a different matter: a 3B cannot fly B-VLOS even though the pilot has a B-VLOS rating.

A 'commercial' drone, duly registered by an operator (section 6), but without an altimeter or the equivalent, will fly R-VLOS.

Indeed, if your drone, registered by your operator, is not fitted with an altimeter or the equivalent, then, although it is 'commercial' (you get paid) you will fly R-VLOS (according to SA-CARS 101.02.3). But the drone must be a Class 4B, spec: 'line-of-sight: any'. All the other non-private Classes – 1C, 2A, 3A, 3B, 4A – carry the specs V-LOS, E-VLOS, B-VLOS, with no mention of R-VLOS.

You need to rely on the operator, who is ultimately responsible for all operations, to do the right thing.

A 'commercial drone' **cannot be flown at night**, except as noted on page 16.

Radio communication: in flying VLOS, E-VLOS and B-VLOS, the pilot must use a registration mark of the drone as a call-sign, must make the required radio calls, indicating altitude, location and intended operation of the drone in that area, and must do so at regular intervals to ensure adequate separation from other aircraft – in short, avoid collisions. A registration mark could be: ZT-BCH (zulu tango bravo charlie hotel).

Scenario of illegal R-VLOS private flying mixed up with commercial

You hold a remote pilot licence (an RPC or an RPL, or even an SRPL – see page 42), but you decide to fly your 3B drone like a privateer, for fun. This is illegal: a 3B 'heavier' drone cannot be flown privately, even in miserable VLOS.

E-VLOS: extended visual line-of-sight

What is 'extended'? According to SACAA: 'An operation below 400 feet above ground level in which an observer maintains direct and unaided visual contact with the remotely piloted aircraft at a distance not exceeding 1 000 metres from the pilot'.

Two handlers are involved: the pilot and the observer (the word 'spotter' is also used).

Of course, because the drone is registered with an operator, the operator must ensure that the observer is fully-trained (also, not younger than 17) and that the communication devices between the pilot and the observer are functional and maintained. There cannot be any lapse in communication since the observer becomes the 'eyes' of the pilot. According to people in the industry, this is an awkward set-up that can work only in optimal conditions. It is onerous on the operator, who must obtain approval from SACAA.

Here it is best to quote SACAA:

> For operations approved for E-VLOS, an operator shall—*(a)* make use of at least one observer who shall not be younger than 17 years of age; and *(b)* ensure that an observer referred to in paragraph *(a)* has completed the training prescribed by an operator in its approved operations manual.

Picture of VLOS and E-VLOS

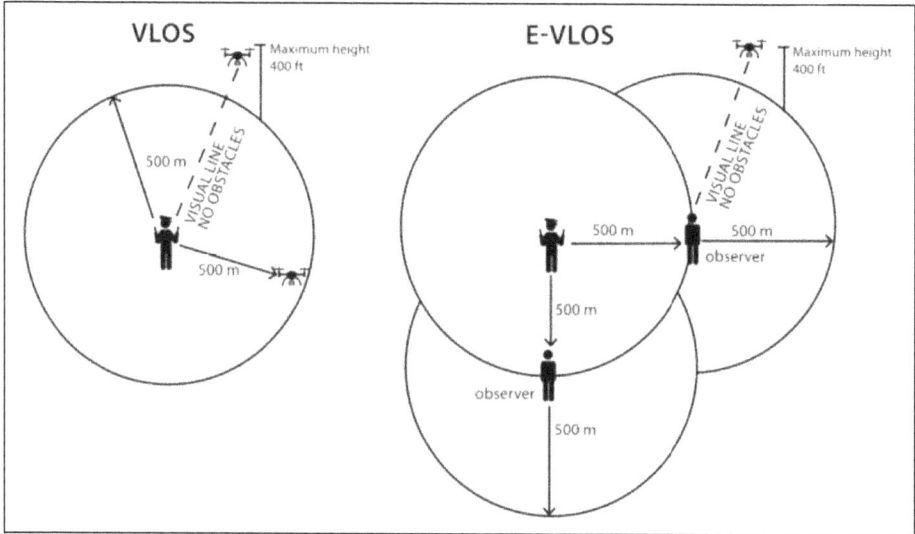

In **clear conditions** the drone can be located up to 1km from you, the licensed pilot, because two persons are involved in managing the drone: you as the 'flying pilot' and further down the line-of-sight, a friend who plays observer and has direct, unaided (binoculars etc are not permitted) LOS of the drone, and stays in touch with you (cellphone is fine), a bit like a navigator who in the grand old age of flying observed the stars to get a position and guide the pilot.

The graphic does not show numerous restrictions, which are taught as part of the training for a licence. The graphic is intended to convey the basic idea of height, distance and vision. E-VLOS does not seem to be very popular at flight schools.

B-VLOS: Beyond visual-line-of-sight

The key component of B-VLOS piloting is the Control and Command link – the so-called C2 link as illustrated below.

Why a 'link'? Because there is no longer a 'line' of sight. The 'line' becomes the 'link'. And the basic visual is replaced by advanced communication technology.

In simple terms (for the uninitiated), the pilot, who cannot see the drone (and without an observer as in E-VLOS) sends, via the C2 link, electronic impulses which trigger actuators which, in turn, trigger the mechanical movements of the drone.

It is up to the operator to provide a robust C2 system. ICAO is clear about it and speaks of a 'link that is robust and ensures reliable operation in all operational circumstances. For the operator to be fully compliant.'

In fact, SACAA places quite a burden on operators for drones to fly B-VLOS.

In B-VLOS operations, the drone is flown outside the pilot's direct visual range, typically relying on technology such as cameras, GPS or sensors to navigate and observe the environment. Technologies for C2 performance are growing more sophisticated by the day to better control the drone so that it performs its tasks optimally, on a predetermined course or a group of waypoints; it can also be interrupted by the pilot for any safety reason.

This means that such a drone flies outside as well as inside controlled airspace, subject to approval by SACAA.

A drone is allowed to **fly at night in B-VLOS** only if the operator, as a UASOC holder (see section 6), has been given approval by SACAA, if it stays below 400ft, and if it has strobe lighting installed. If it is an aeroplane, it must have navigation lights (green R, red L, white Tail) and if it is a helicopter or multi-rotor, it must have a beacon light.

In addition, it can fly only in two categories of controlled airspace, ATZ and CTR (put simply, around and above an aerodrome or in the wider volume of an airport), and in clear weather (visual meteorological conditions, VMC), always below 400ft. The take-away is that, unless your certified operator gets permission from SACAA, flying drones at that level of competency is not do-as-you-please.

I am giving these details, which are taught in RPC and RPL training, to illustrate how restrictive the rules are.

A pilot who holds a B-VLOS rating must be able to make radio calls and report the drone's identity, current position and altitude, and next intended operation – all in real time, to any other aircraft or to an Air Traffic Service Unit (a 'tower'). Hence the mandatory radio certificate licences that form part of the RPC and the RPL.

B-VLOS is the future

In short, if you are getting licensed, get a B-VLOS rating at the same time.

BVLOS is particularly valuable for inspecting large-scale facilities, remote infrastructure or hazardous areas where maintaining a direct line of sight is impractical.

B-VLOS leveraged by industry has several challenges: safety, privacy, integration in airspace, traffic management, robust long-range communication technology, specialised training of pilots and developing jobs for large data management – what is the point of large data collecting if it cannot be analysed fully and rapidly? It is the future of civilian drones, and is becoming an industry on its own, spawning all sorts of other ventures.

Here is ICAO's neat summary on the applicability of B-VLOS:

BVLOS UAS Operations – operational type	Example
Near BVLOS • Localized 'wide' area survey • Blocked from remote pilot view (building, tree, terrain)	• Small/medium agriculture or survey • Fire, Police, EMS
Remote area BVLOS	• Outback agriculture • Arctic/Antarctic survey
Linear survey/patrol	Rail corridor, pipelines, electrical lines
Wide area survey	Mining, oil and gas
Cargo delivery (urban, rural)	Wing, Zipline

(Source: ICAO)

B-VLOS is becoming a top consideration for an operator (which pays you, the pilot, to fly) when an extended range is necessary, for example, land surveying or flying over large or distant agricultural, industrial, mining sites, power lines and wind turbines, or infrastructure inspection where obstacles prevent a continuous VLOS. Operators want a survey that is as complete as possible, without blind spots, with high resolution images, saving also on the costs of having several E-VLOS pilots and observers scattered on the terrain.

Here is a pictogram – but it will not teach you much; only training for a licence will.

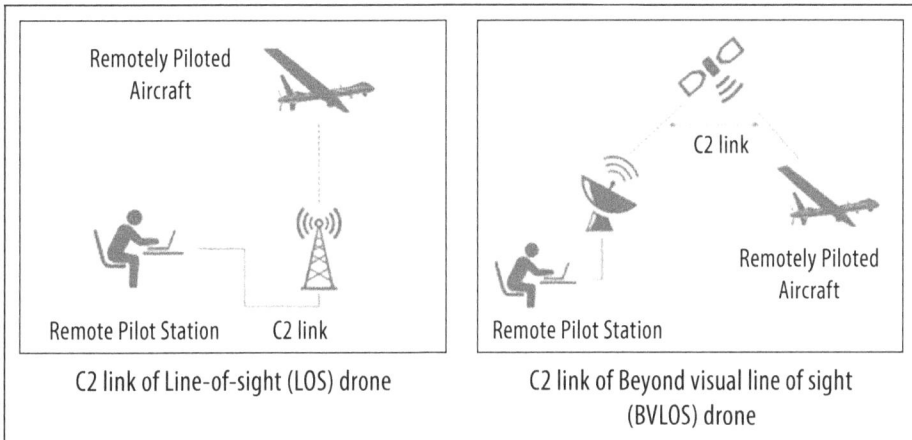

| C2 link of Line-of-sight (LOS) drone | C2 link of Beyond visual line of sight (BVLOS) drone |

And now, what you've been waiting for: licences. We have dealt with drones fit to fly commercially, dealt with what drones can do, and provided some information about operators. What remains from the three 'commercial' points highlighted at the beginning of this section are you, the pilot, and your licence.

What are remote pilot licences?

There is no word, in aviation, that is used as proudly as 'pilot'. It carries prestige. You have your wings or you don't. This is also true in the brave new world of drones. Unless you hold a 'licence', you are not a true pilot.

The problem is that not all licences are called licences (not to mention the spelling).

The categories of 'commercial' remote pilot licences

To avoid a bun fight at the traditional Saturday morning breakfast at your local aeroclub, here is an important SACAA Notice issued on 26 March 2023.

'South Africa has adopted a Remote Pilot Certificate for UAS operation defined under Part 71'. Note that SACAA uses 'UAS' not 'RPAS'. UAS is used more internationally.

What SACAA is defining here is **the licence called the RPC or the Remote Pilot Certificate**. Part 71 of the Regulations and Standards (SA-CARS and SA-CATS) deals with the RPC. It is, as a pilot, your reference.

There will be a bun fight anyway at the aeroclub, so check this:

In South Africa, there are, legally, **three types of licences** for remote pilots; in addition, there is still, but not for long, one **'old' licence**.

The three current licences

The **Remote Pilot Certificate**, or **RPC**. It is the 'licence' (not in word but in reality) that a remote pilot must get if flying privately is not enough. Flying commercially begins here. **Most pilots as of today go for the RPC.**

The **Remote Pilot Licence**, or **RPL**, is an advanced licence that builds on the RPC.

The **Student Remote Pilot Licence**, or **SRPL**. You hold it while you are training for the **RPL**. It is a licence valid only during training for the RPL.

The old licence pre-2023

In March 2023 SACAA changed the RPAS pilot licensing and its terminology. Until then, the RPL was the only licence. When SACAA's system was brought more in line with international standards, the **RPC replaced the pre-2023 RPL**, and a new RPL was introduced. **In plain English: when you renew your old RPL, if you have one, you'll get an RPC**. Your flight school will advise you. The old RPL has been discontinued.

There is no 'Student Remote Pilot Certificate'

But the regulations speak of a 'student remote pilot' in training at a flight school to obtain an RPC.

All these licences, whether 'certificate' or 'licence', follow strict legal rules and they grant you rights of how to fly and where and what for. Flying rights are called 'privileges' in aviation, but they carry 'limitations'.

Take no notice of SACAA using the American spelling of 'licence' ('license') here and there; it is untidy but makes no difference to what the licences are.

SACAA's notice adds, and do not get confused:

'**Remote Pilot Licenses** [it should be 'licences'] **specific to drones** [it should be 'UAS', to be consistent] **operated internationally and within instrument flight conditions** [it should be 'under instrument flight rules'] **aligned with Annex 14** [of ICAO] **has been defined under Part 72**.

Part 72? This is **the new RPL or the Remote Pilot Licence** and, so far, the only one at that level, although the Notice uses the (misspelt) plural 'licenses'. Part 72 of SA-CARS and SA-CATS (currently incomplete) deals with the (new) RPL.

> **ALERT!** Some drone websites have not updated their information: on some, the currently legal Remote Pilot Certificate is called by its old name 'Remote Pilot Licence'. Others mention a 'Remote Pilot Competency' and use 'RPC' as if it is the RPC listed here; it is not the same thing (for 'competency' see page 61). Some, knowing about the change of rules and the newly established RPC, refer to a 'Remote Proficiency Certificate', which looks like the current RPC. Don't worry: you will enrol for the new, current, unique RPC (section 4). And if you want to up your game, you will need the new RPL (section 5).

Watch out for 'RPC' or 'RPL' used overseas

In Australia an RPL is not a remote pilot licence; it refers to a 'Recreational Pilot Licence' and has nothing to do with a South African RPL. However, Australia offers a remote pilot licence abbreviated 'RePL', and the specs are as different from our RPL as a kangaroo is from a springbok.

In the United States a 'Recreational Pilot Certificate' is not drone-specific. But its 'Remote Pilot Certificate', hardly ever abbreviated RPC, is commonly called a 'license', and it is close enough to our RPC.

In the European Union: Sweden, for example, issues a remote pilot Certificate of Competency, translated in their variety of globalised English as a 'drone license'. It is required to operate any drone with a MTOM of 250g or more. Tough.

In Canada, there are three drone pilot certificates: Level 1 Basic Operations corresponds roughly to private flying in SA. So, if you take your drone to Québec, for private flying, you'll need that Level 1 Certificate over there (in French, of course). Levels 2 and 3 are Advanced Operations and Special Flight Operations and seem to correspond to our RPC and RPL.

Japan refers, in translation, to 'Classes' of 'UAV' licences. As of October 2024, nearly 20,000 licences have been granted in the Empire of the Rising Sun and home of the inspiring aviator's manga and movie, *Kaze Tachinu, The Wind Has Risen*.

The UK asks that remote pilots begin by getting a Flyer ID (with a test), and then they progress to obtain an A2 Certificate of Competency (CofC) or a General VLOS Certificate (GVC). Two more qualifications are at a planning stage.

Botswana, Namibia, Zimbabwe: see section 7.

Why mention all of this? If while on holiday overseas you want to fly your drone, don't take for it granted that licences, or just handling a drone, that carry the same acronym or sound the same refer to the same type of South African products and practices. Don't assume. Check. In some countries you simply cannot fly any drone at all.

In any event, without being licensed wherever you are abroad, you won't be able to fly without adhering to the rules in place there. Even 'private' drone flying can lead to problems, because national rules do vary. And the reverse is true for **foreigners coming to SA**, for a film shoot, for instance: read this guide before sending your drone aloft. But tourists who come to South Africa are really lucky that they have the freedom to fly light drones privately – provided they follow the rules (section 2).

Let us now look at what the pilot in you wants to read about: the RPC.

Section 4

The Remote Pilot Certificate (RPC)

This section introduces you to the rule-based world of remote pilot licensing. It will give you a clear idea of what you are letting yourself in for, should you decide to become – and you should – a proper drone pilot.

Reading what follows will prepare you to take a major step forward, which is to enrol and get licensed.

South Africa has one of the longest flying histories, almost on par with pioneering countries. Training received at our **Aviation Training Organisations** (ATOs) – in plain English, flight schools – is of an international standard, and our pilots are sought after world-wide. I am giving you all these details below so that you can decide for yourself if you want to register at an ATO and undergo training. You should.

When you get your RPC you can call yourself a licensed remote pilot, and you can fly commercially. Never mind the word 'certificate'. The RPC is a licence and you are licensed. Most licensed remote pilots who fly commercially hold the RPC. And, when you get it, you can pin wings on your pilot shirt (left breast pocket). If you have one. You should have one.

But, before that: training. Let's proceed step by step.

Although this overview is detailed, it is for information only. It cannot replace formal instruction at a SACAA-approved ATO. It is meant to prep you for making the move.

Step 1: Enrolling at an ATO

You need to enrol at a SACAA-approved ATO. You cannot study theory or train practically on your own. You may get tuition online, but you have to enrol at an ATO. You may also see a different acronym for ATO (there are more acronyms in aviation than there are pilots): RTO. Don't take any notice.

What ATOs are on the market, which are approved by SACAA?

As at May 2025, 226 ATOs are listed on SACAA's dedicated page; some are noted to have 'expired', and only a few offer drone training. For each ATO listed, the menu of their training offerings is provided. This does not mean that they actually run all courses. It means that SACAA has approved it.

Here is the otherwise hard-to-get-at URL that should lead you directly to a complete list of ATOs. Once you get there, just type in your location, and see what comes up: https://www.caa.co.za/approved-training-organizations/ (this not a permalink).

There is also a list of ATOs that specialise in remote licensing, but it was last updated in July 2024. Follow on the SACAA website: Industry>Personnel licensing>Training and scroll down to List of Remote Pilot Aviation Training Organisations. The link (not a permalink) to the list is: https://caasanwebsitestorage.blob.core.windows.net/aviation-personnel-standards/RPC%20ATO%20List.pdf

You can contact SACAA: clientcare@caa.co.za, 0860 267 435, or email PEL.Training@caa.co.za

This is what an ATO's offering looks like (real case, name hidden) on the general online list of ATOs:

Approved Training Organisation Certificate	
Radio Telephone (Restricted)	2019-06-03
RPC – Instructor Rating	2019-06-03
RPC (A) – B-VLOS	2019-12-12
RPC (A) – VLOS	2019-06-03
RPC (MR) – B-VLOS	2019-12-12
RPC (MR) – VLOS	2019-06-03
RPL – Instructor Rating	2019-06-03

As you can see, this ATO is offering training for the RPC (A) with a VLOS or B-VLOS rating; the RPC (MR), quadcopter in drone language, same ratings, but no RPC (H). It does not specify which machines they are licensed to operate, so you will have to ask. You may not like them. Make sure you make the right choice, of category of course, and even of machines.

Some practical advice

Beware of scamming: An ATO must be certified by SACAA; if certified, it must have a currently valid certification. When you look up the URL mentioned, you'll see a red dot for invalid ATOs. If in doubt, email PEL.Training@caa.co.za

Choose your school carefully: Visit a flight school close to you, check it out, see if the age range of the trainees fits your profile, and if the office and classroom have a good feel. Ask how many remote pilots got their licences with them. And talk to whoever will be your instructor. All that matters. It must be a happy and rewarding investment of your time and your money.

SACAA has a useful guidance document that may be overdoing it because it is aimed at manned aviation trainees. You will find *How to choose the right aviation training school* on the same page as Industry>Personnel licensing>Training, scroll down to Training Organisation Information.

On the subject of money: Ask what the ATO fees are, what they actually cover, what the fees for testing are, and what SACAA fees you can be expected to pay in addition. Sit down with your instructor and draw up a budget, all inclusive of ATO fees for registration, material, classes, flying; medical certificate fees; language proficiency test fees; SACAA's numerous fees for annual currency, exams, issuing of licences; and ask about instructor's and examiner's fees.

If, for some reason, you need more hours, your budget will have to be adjusted. Some pilots see expenses mount and are not too happy about it.

The small print: Make sure you read the Ts and Cs about interrupting your studies, cancelling, and a refund if you paid an amount upfront.

Ask about insurance: Are you covered for breakage of a drone, for causing an injury to a person or damage to property? The aviation insurance industry provides for pilots; ask your ATO.

What category of drones can you be licensed for?

You have read above what **Classes of UAS, or drones**, can be flown commercially. Now you must decide **what 'category' of UAS** you want to be licensed for, which also depends on the offerings at the ATO of your choice.

A category is not a Class

Classes are defined by flying altitude, energy and 'weight' (see section 2).

Categories are defined by the engineering design of the aircraft.

There are three categories of UAS/drones:

- UAS aeroplane (A)
- UAS helicopter (H)
- UAS multirotor (MR)

Why? Because a drone is an engine-powered heavier-than-air aircraft, unlike a glider for instance (to keep it simple), it can only be an aeroplane or a rotorcraft (the wings are rotary, that is the blades) capable of vertical take-off (VTOL); in plain English: helicopter or multirotor (in drone lingo: quadcopter, etc).

So, when you decide to train for the RPC, you have to choose which category you want for your licence: do you want an RPC (A) or (H) or (MR). You cannot get the three together. **Each category has its own licensing and its own training** – although most of the general theoretical knowledge overlaps, for example, meteorology. Your RPC will be issued RPC (A), RPC (H) or RPC (MR).

Not all ATOs offer the three RPCs. So, when choosing your RPC, you will have to decide which one you want, and also check what the ATO offers.

The choice you are going to make therefore depends on what drones your ATO operates, and what training it is licensed for.

Remember that you cannot do the training privately.

How long does it take?

The better question is how many hours of tuition and practical training are needed to complete and get your RPC, or what the actual average completion time is. Age plays a role; don't fool yourself. Drone flying demands quick reactions.

With regard to the actual flying, the skills, ask how many hours is the average, and if the flying that you've done privately can help you to speed things up. Then you can get to the Skills Test more quickly.

Your own allocation of time may depend on the scheduling of lectures and training sessions: some ATOs hold 'theoretical' classes as a block of lectures, others spread them out. Some do one-on-one lessons, at your convenience. Make sure you find out about the possibilities. Some ATOs run the courses online, and they work. But having an instructor in front of you has its own advantages, and you can feel that you 'belong'. That part in aviation is traditionally called 'ground school'.

Try to stay with the same instructor, and avoid changing flight schools.

Once you have signed up, your ATO should take care of everything, from study material to well-maintained drones, to getting you ready for the final test, and helping you to fill in the 'swarm' of SACAA forms. Be ready to pay what SACAA demurely calls 'applicable fees', for this and that, and whatnot. Fees change every year and are advertised by SACAA, and your ATO should tell you.

The next step, and your ATO should see to it, is for you to pass your 'medical'.

Step 2: Getting your 'medical'

No medical, no training.

It is a big one. All pilots need a medical certification. No 'medical', no licence, no flying.

Bottom line: you have to be healthy (and stay healthy), and be declared healthy. This is not as straightforward as it seems.

You need a medical Class 3 or III

A higher medical is fine, but a Class 3 or III is what you need (3 or III are the two ways of writing it).

Your ATO should send you to a Designated Aviation Medical Examiner, called a DAME, before taking your full fees, if applicable, just in case you fail your 'medical', or your ATO should provide for a refund in such a case. In fact, check the 'small print' for what sort of refund you can expect for an upfront payment if you fail your 'medical'. If you are declared medically unfit, you cannot proceed with training and your ATO is very aware of that. ATOs are honourable.

Your ATO will give you the names of SACAA-certified medical doctors. **Your own GP won't do,** unless he or she is a DAME. For a Class 3 or III a Senior DAME is mandatory as 'Class I & III Medical Certificate can only be issued by Senior DAMEs', according to the law.

There is a **cost** involved and it can be expensive, depending upon the DAME. Don't be reluctant to ask how much, and shop around. While it is an essential service to aviation, it is also a lucrative business. You are a paying customer, not a worried patient.

Once you select a DAME and you are happy with the quality of service, it is a good idea to stay with that practitioner for the next time (in 24 months actually).

What does a Class 3 or III 'medical' involve?

Here are the headings, to give you an idea of the protocols involved, and the checklist that the DAME must follow:

- Physical and mental standards (Psychiatric, Neurological, Musculo-skeletal, Gastrointestinal, Respiratory, Cardiovascular, Metabolic, Nutritional and Endocrine, Haematologic and Immunologic, Genitourinary, Oncology)
- Visual standards (especially Near vision and intermediate vision, Distance vision, Dioptre limits)
- Ear, nose and throat and hearing standards
- Electro-cardiography
- Flow Volume Lung Function

Some things to watch out for

Psychology: When a DAME starts the session with small talk, be aware that since the Germanwings Flight 9525 disaster-by-suicide in March 2015, aviation regulators have woken up to the risks posed by mental issues. In 2024, only nine years later, SACAA introduced a fresh battery of mental checks, under Schedule 49 Mental Health Conditions.

While chatting, some DAMEs are observing your behaviour. It is a casual way of assessing you – in addition to specific questions ('Any anxiety issues?'). If asked, explain clearly why you want to be a remote pilot; don't brag, just be yourself. Answer factual questions truthfully and factually.

Eyewear: Do you wear glasses? Corrective lenses are acceptable to your DAME; this is not an issue provided the testing goes well, but **remember to take them with you** when you go to your medical. Many pilots fly with glasses, and not only green-tinted Ray-Bans.

Don't fret, don't lie: The examination will flow with ease. The DAME will ask you questions about any problems you have had, recent (or not recent) surgery, if you take medication, if you sleep well, if you drink, what and how much, and will also conduct tests (such as vision, audio). The first time it will be intimidating, but it will flow. Don't lie: if you cause an accident and it is discovered that you had a condition that you did not disclose, you will be in real trouble.

When you make your appointment it is a good idea to double-check whether there will be a **blood test** at the DAME's rooms or clinic, and, if so, whether you should fast beforehand and for how long. Expect to provide a urine sample.

Outcome? Good to go, of course. If there is a problem, the DAME will explain what it is, and suggest remedial action, or refer you to a specialist and declare you temporarily unfit until a remedy has been applied (in that case, the report goes to the Aeromedical Committee of SACAA for further action). Trust your DAME and ask 'what next?'

If for some reason you are unwell, rather postpone the examination.

Nowadays, the tests and results are captured electronically on a platform, called EMPIC, and sent directly to SACAA (or they should be).

How long is a medical valid for?

There are three scenarios, depending on your age

Don't confuse it with the time validity of your coveted RPC (24 months). The time validity of your medical may not coincide with that of your licensing.

You are under 40 years: Your 'medical' is valid for 48 months calculated from the last day of the calendar month in which the medical certificate is issued.

You are over 40 : The validity is 24 months. This means that it will be valid for the period of validity of your RPC (but beware of the syncing of dates).

Over 50: The validity is 12 months. A bummer: half-way through the validity of your RPC, you have to get a new medical. If you don't, you can't fly.

Please don't confuse 'calendar year' with '12 months'. Some pilots have been heard to say: 'I got my medical in 2025, next is in 2027'. No.

Step 3: The English Language Proficiency Certificate

You must be fluent in English, and prove it. This has snagged some trainee pilots, so don't be careless about it.

Your aim is to secure a 6 ('levels of proficiency' are explained on page 55).

Do it as soon as you can. Again, check what provision is made in your contract with the ATO about a refund if you fail to get a mark of at least 4, because you can't get licensed if your mark is below 4.

There are **three ways of securing** your English Language Proficiency Certificate.

Scenario 1: You will not have to be tested for fluency in English, if:

- you can prove you have Matric, O or M level, with a pass in English first language with a minimum of D or its equivalent – if so, you'll get a 6 rating, valid for life.
- you can prove you have a nationally (SAQA) recognised two-year tertiary qualification with English as a subject or English as a teaching and examination language – rated 6 for life.
- you are (or have been) a national of a state where English is the first language (UK, USA, etc) – rated 6 for life.

'For life' means that you will not have to be tested again.

Scenario 2: You have been already tested by a foreign CAA as per ICAO directive

The result that you got there will be accepted by SACAA here.

If you are unhappy about your foreign rating, then you can get re-tested here, in the hope that you'll get a top 6.

Beware of playing games: imagine you got a 5 overseas in a non-English speaking country where the examiners believe they are fluent in English, and you re-test here to get a better 6, and then you land up with a 4 ... you'll be very sorry.

In any re-test (or exam re-marking by SACAA for that matter), the latest rating prevails.

Scenario 3: You test for a Certificate of Competency in ICAO English Language Proficiency

Your ATO will organise your test or send you to an Approved Test Centre, which may or may not be at your ATO.

At the test, first you'll fill in a Bio-Data Questionnaire, and then you'll undergo an Oral Proficiency Interview with two examiners: a Subject Matter Expert (in aviation) and a Linguistic Expert (in English). The test is about 45 minutes face-to-face.

How does the test work?

The two examiners will look out for:

Pronunciation: Ability to speak in a manner that is clear and easy to understand.

Structure: Ability to compose concise, meaningful and unambiguous sentences or messages.

Vocabulary: Ability to use correct words and phrases to match the setting.

Fluency: Ability to respond, narrate events or describe situations naturally.

Comprehension: Ability to understand and follow instructions without difficulty.

Interaction: Ability to ask and answer questions, and engage in two-way dialogue without difficulty.

Remember that the **Aviation Expert** will want to hear that you know the aviation lingo, while the **English Linguist** will want to make sure that you can speak good, everyday English.

You will be rated as having one of the following levels of proficiency:

Proficiency Level	Proficiency Testing Interval
Level 6: Expert	Retesting not required
Level 5: Extended	Retesting required every six years
Level 4: Operational (Minimum level)	Retesting required every three years
Level 3: Pre-operational	Licence not issued/maintained
Level 2: Elementary	Licence not issued/maintained
Level 1: Pre-elementary	Licence not issued/maintained

You must get a 6 rating.

If you get a 5, you'll have to do it again after six years; if a 4, every third year. A 6 is for life.

If you are disappointed by a 5 or a 4, and you want a better rating, get re-assessed after 90 days (at a cost, of course). If you get a worse rating, be careful: this new one counts, not the first one.

Syncing licensing and proficiency re-testing

If you don't get a 6, but a 5 or 4, it can get a bit complicated in terms of syncing the revalidation of your RPC (every 24 months) with, for example, a triennial level 4 re-testing. Imagine you get your RPC, and you are language rated 4. After 24 months you revalidate your initial RPC, but a year later the proficiency test is now due again. Not to mention that, if you are 50+, you would have your third medical that year. It gets busy.

Best advice: get a 6.

If you get a 1, 2 or 3, the licence cannot be issued

There are remedial actions that the Test Centre must make available to you. Again, wait 90 days to re-test. Until you move to 4, your licence will not be issued.

Advice: do the test as early as you can, and see what the small print in your contract with the ATO says about a refund if you cannot get past level 3. Get advice from your instructor when you have a chat before enrolling.

Fees: SACAA and both examiners will charge you.

And now, let us look at how you get there, which is part of what you must submit as proof to SACAA when you fill in the RPC application form (see page 59).

Step 4: Ground school

After enrolling, ground school begins – it is called Step 4 here for convenience's sake. But if you fail your medical, you can't proceed. And if you fail your English test, or if your English is shaky, you can't really begin ground school.

'Ground school' is the traditional aviation expression for following classes about theory at a flight school. **It is the 'academic' part of your training**. It follows a syllabus and its outcome is a general, written examination.

At ground school you will be taught an academic syllabus

The syllabus replicates that of manned aircraft pilots, in the five standard areas of aviation theory (see the detailed syllabus on page 81):

- Air law
- Human factors
- Meteorology
- Navigation and flight planning
- Technical aspects, some specific to the drone that you are going to be licensed for.

Based on the syllabus, your ATO will set and mark your one and only 'theoretical knowledge examination', which is called a 'general examination'. Multiple choice questions will cover the five areas mentioned. Some pilots do struggle with it, but with a good instructor and some steady studying it should be fine. Your ATO will see to it.

The pass mark is 75%

If you fail, you can rewrite, but various rules apply; your ATO will advise. It is set and marked at your ATO. If SACAA decides to organise it at a Test Centre, your ATO will inform you about booking a slot.

As a remote pilot, you need to remember that the regulations (SA-CARS) and applicable standards (SA-CATS) for drones are **Parts 71, 72 and 101. Remember these numbers**: it may be an exam question. Remember also that Medical is Part 67.

You must pass the examination within 90 days (not three calendar months) of the Skills Test. Put differently: when you sit the general exam, make sure you are getting ready to do the practical Skills Test soon.

Restricted Radiotelephony Certificate

At some stage during ground school you will have to get it. 'Charlie-Tango-Bravo'? Not quite, but you will need to pass a 'restricted aeronautical radiotelephony certificate'. Your ATO will train you (over a day or two) for the test. The exam comprises a theory exam and an oral exam.

It is a serious part of your training for a RPC. Most trainees enjoy it. And it is quite valuable too: if you decide to get a Private Pilot Licence (on a 'real' aircraft), you will already have your radio.

Step 5: Flight training and the Skills Test

As you start ground school you'll also start practising your flying skills. This is the flight training part. It leads to the 'Skills Test', which rounds off your entire training, and hopefully gives you your RPC.

If you go for an RPC (A) (aeroplane), you'll train with an equivalent drone, and get tested with it. That is the Skills Test. In the same way, a manned aviation pilot is tested A and not H (helicopter), if the pursued licence is a Private Pilot Licence (A), for argument's sake.

SACAA reminds us that the Skills Test must 'include the applicable sections for E-VLOS or B-VLOS rating', as you chose to train. VLOS is the standard.

Flying skills for the Skills Test

See page 85 for precisely what flying skills are demanded of you: it is the Skills Test marking sheet used by examiners. These are in fact the skills you will learn with your instructor. Each item represents the flight training that you did: it is a checklist and a grading of skills.

Your aim in the Skills Test is to score 3s or 4s throughout.

Marking sheet

The **examiner follows the Skills Test marking sheet.** It is thorough and, as mentioned, it replicates every single skill that you have been taught and that you must master to become a licensed remote pilot. All pilots go through this gruelling experience; you are no exception.

Example of an unsuccessful test: If you score a poor 2 for 'Fly a square box rotating the MR in the direction of flight' (skill 7.9), then you'll be asked to do that manoeuvre again, now, not tomorrow, and you have only one chance. If you get a 2 again, it is back to training. You must get a 3, at least.

That is why it is a good idea to refer to the Skills Test marking sheet as you advance in your practical training – to see where you stand. Your instructor will debrief you after each flight, grade your progress, and make a record that is signed off. You can, of course, challenge a debrief, but challenging an examiner is never a good idea …

At the end, before your test, your ATO will actually certify that you completed your flight training. Until your instructor is sure that you are ready to test, you won't be allowed to test.

Timing of the test: You must test no more than 60 days (not two calendar months) after completing your flight instruction.

Usually no one gets a good night's sleep before a Skills Test. You'll become a pilot, and then you can sleep.

Step 6: Applying for the RPC

Once you have passed it all, you can **formally apply to get that coveted licence** (see the form on page 91).

'Applying' is confusing

This is not about 'applying to an ATO', in the same way as you apply to varsity, that is, before you start studying. No, it is about filling in an application form to have SACAA deliver your licence, the RPC, **once you have completed your full training and passed the final exams (paper plus skills, plus all that is mandatory, as mentioned above)**.

There is no registration with SACAA when you start training. Once you are done with the entire training, and passed your Skills Test, then you apply. The RPL (section 5) is another matter because of the Student Remote Pilot Licence.

You must be 18 years old when you apply for the RPC

The logic is that you can start ground school and practical training before you are 18, but you must be 18 when you fill in the application form. But **you can only fill in that form after you have completed all that is mandatory in terms of training and related matters, and you must supply proof.**

The application, requirements and proofs

Check both the Requirements form (see page 92) as well as the Application form currently valid (see page 91): there is a detailed list of what must be submitted together with your application form or what must be on the record (medical).

The following items are mandatory, must be secured before you test anyway, and proof must be provided:

- a valid medical certificate Class 3 or III
- a restricted radio certificate of proficiency in radiotelephony (aeronautical)
- a certificate of English proficiency level 4 or higher

- proof of written examination passed (that is your theoretical part of your training)
- proof that you have completed the flight training requirement provided by your ATO
- the Skills Test form signed by an appropriate examiner/instructor and the result of the test marked on the Skills Test form
- a copy of the last three pages of **your logbook** with a record of flight time (every pilot has a logbook)

About your pilot logbook

Your instructor will show you how to record every single flight. Never write over, erase or 'Tipp-Ex' over any entry in your logbook. Rather photocopy a dummy page, use it to draft the new entry, check that it is correct, and then make the entry. Use a black pen only. Get into the habit of making the entry after each flight.

If you do this electronically, print pages every 90 days.

After the end of your RPC validity, keep your logbook for 60 months.

- there is a SACAA fee, needless to say (your ATO will advise on the current amount)
- sending the application: usually your ATO will do it on your behalf, by courier, if you give them permission to do so.

The next step: maintain and revalidate your RPC

You are allowed to fly for gain, 'commercially', but only nationally

Fly, get a job, but only within the borders and airspace of 'the Republic'.

About the borders of 'the Republic': Let us assume that your operator is allowed to operate drones over (not to and from) Marion Island, far away in the South Atlantic. This is legal because the two Prince Edward Islands, and the Antarctica station, are part of 'the Republic'. If your operator manages to get permission for you to fly into Botswana or Namibia and secures the required authorisations from the foreign civil aviation authorities concerned, you should be fine. Otherwise, stay national. Stay legal.

If you fly illegally, you risk getting suspended or losing your RPC (apart from any criminal case that may be brought against you).

Pay your currency fee due to SACAA

All fees are updated effective every 1 April (see page 93). They never decrease. Check the SACAA website, Industry>Personnel Licensing>Fees (no permalink). Email: clientcare@caa.co.za

SACAA is moving to a two-year upfront fee system, but it is unclear whether this has been rolled out for RPC, SRPL and RPL. Check with your ATO or with SACAA client care.

Maintain competency and revalidate

Your **RPC must be revalidated before the 24 months of current validity expire**, that is, your RPC is valid until the last day of the 24th month from the date of issue (the SACAA date on your licence). This is not two calendar years. To be precise:

- **You must revalidate within 90 days (not three months) before the date of expiry** of your RPC. You can do it ahead of those 90 days, but the new date of issue will be the last day of the month in which the revalidation test is passed (you do it on 1 March, the issuance date will be 31 March … so think twice before playing a calendar game).
- **Only an ATO can help you to revalidate** because only an ATO can organise the revalidation test. The aim is to check if you have retained competency or even improved on it – go to the Skills Test form and look at the grading: again, aim for a 4, which means 'excellent'.
- You may be asked, for instance, to fly a couple of sorties before the test if your logbook shows that **you have not flown enough 'recently'** and if the instructor who will prep you thinks you are not ready for the revalidation test and are at risk of scoring a 2 at any skill tested, which means you will fail.

- **You will redo the initial Skills Test. Look at the form** (pages 85–90).
- The paperwork **must be submitted to SACAA within 30 days** (not one calendar month) of the test (if you pass, which you will – if not, the ATO will advise on remedial action).
- Remember that **you need a valid 'medical'.**
- If applicable, you need **a valid English proficiency rating**.

Of course, you will have to pay **fees** for the test and to SACAA.

Remember: No valid RPC, no valid medical, no flying.

Now, as a SA remote pilot licensed holder, can you legally and commercially fly 'internationally'? No, to fly a drone 'internationally', you will need an RPL.

Section 5

The New Remote
Pilot Licence (RPL)

As already explained, up to 2023, there was a Remote Pilot Licence (RPL), which is now called the Remote Pilot Certificate (RPC). This section deals with the new RPL.

Pilots who hold the pre-2023 'old' RPL will get an RPC when they re-validate their old RPL (the last ones should be in 2025).

Some flight school websites are not very clear about it, although they know the difference. So be aware of 'RPL' being used to mean the 'old' RPL.

In this section, RPL means the RPL introduced in 2023. It is an advanced licence, and is the only one (with the student's RPL or SRPL) that is properly called a 'licence' (SACAA also uses, of late, the American spelling 'license', but it does not matter).

This RPL is new and ATOs are still developing their training manuals. This situation is not specific to South Africa; it is a global situation in civil aviation.

The RPL is definitely the future of the pilot profession and of the industry alongside fully automated (no pilot needed) long distance flying vehicles which often look like manned aeroplanes or helicopters, and are not true drones because they are fully automated, that is, without even a remote pilot. But let us not get bogged down by terminology that even national civil aviation bodies have not yet really sorted out, as we saw at the beginning of this guide.

The details provided here take the form of Q&As. It is a different format from that of section 4 because the new RPL is not yet fully developed in terms of legislation. Few ATOs offer it, even if they are certified by SACAA to operate and train.

Q&As about the new RPL

This is advanced piloting. Nonetheless, we all have to end somewhere. So here is a list of the basic queries that come to mind:

Q: What is the basic difference between an RPC and an RPL?

A: You need an RPL to fly internationally under IFR.

Q: What does 'internationally' mean?

A: 'Internationally' does not mean that you can use your RPL abroad. It means that, subject to your operator having done the necessary, you can remotely fly your drone across the borders of 'the Republic' and away from non-South African airspace. This is ICAO's wording: An international flight is 'a flight stage with one or both terminals in the territory of a State, other than the State in which the air carrier has its principal place of business'. A flight that is not 'international' is domestic. And this is SACAA's different version: '**international flight** means a flight which passes through the airspace over the territory of more than one State'.

Q: What is IFR?

A: IFR stands for Instrument Flight Rules.

In manned aviation a pilot who is flying will change from visual rules to IFR if, for instance, very bad weather (called: Instrument Meteorological Conditions (IMC)) occurs, provided that the pilot has an instrument rating and the 'tower' allows the pilot to change over to IFR. My example looks simple to seasoned pilots. Just remember that flying a drone under IFR is a complex affair if you are not already a professional pilot in manned aviation, and excellent at the game of complex remote controlling.

Q: IFR is one step up, then.

A: Yes, with IFR you are now in a totally different game. The theoretical training is specific and similar to that of a manned aircraft professional pilot, in addition to which you will be trained, and tested, in the management of complex C2 links – the electronics that allow you to remotely command, control and manage a drone that is flying without you being able to see it (to put it simply again), somewhere out there.

Q: Can I fly a massive quad then?

A: Actually not a massive quad, nor any quad. The RPL is awarded only in categories (A) and (H). There is no category (MR), what people often call a quad. And the RPL only applies to drones, either (A) or (H), that weigh between 25 kg and 150 kg.

Q: Hold on, in the classification, there is Class 4B?

Class 3A	BVLOS	E > 34	h < 400	m < 150
Class 3B	VLOS/EVLOS	Any	h > 400	m < 150
Class 4A	BVLOS	Any	h > 400	m < 150
Class 4B	Any	Any	Any	m > 150

A: Good point. But then you have to do specialised training called a 'type rating' (at an ATO) before you can use your RPL (A) or (H) with a Class 4B.

Q: You mentioned an operator?

A: As with an RPC, if you want to fly for gain, you need to do it under a certified operator (or be a certified operator). See section 6.

Q: How old must I be?

A: As in the case of an RPC, you must be 18 years of age at the time you apply for your licence ie right after you pass your Skills Test (and provided you hold all that is required).

Q: What about that student licence, SRPL?

A: When you enrol at an ATO, you automatically apply for a SRPL, and you must be at least 17 years old. You will need a medical certificate 3 or III and be proficient in English. As for an RPC, the ATO will organise the paperwork.

The only difference between you aiming for an RPL and someone training for an RPC is that you will hold a licence, the SPRL, and have the formal status of a 'student pilot'. Your SPRL is valid for two years (24 months, not two calendar years).

Q: Is the SPRL valid for two years?

A: Yes, which means that SACAA believes it can take you up to two years to get fully trained and pass all the exams before you get to the RPL Skills Test.

Q: If I already have an RPC, can I get credit for it?

A: Don't be unrealistic. In terms of handling, it may help you shave off a couple of flying hours, and save some expenses. But it is entirely at your ATO's discretion. But remember the IFR issue: RPC training will not really prepare you for that sort of piloting. And, with regard to theory, you must pass (or must have passed if you hold a commercial (CPL) or airline (ATPL) licence) CPL or ATPL theoretical knowledge examinations and, of course, the instrument rating theoretical examination.

It is serious. It will also bring you serious money later.

Q: Anything else, like radiotelephony?

A: Yes, spot on. You need a **general aeronautical radiotelephony certificate**. Your ATO will advise and set you up. The RPC restricted certificate will not do.

Q: And then I am done – RPL for life?

A: No. Twelve months after the date of issue of your RPL, you must revalidate ie get tested again. And thereafter the same, while keeping your medical Class 3 or III valid (see page 50). And, if you don't have a 6 in English proficiency, make sure you re-do the test when needed (see page 53).

Section 6

Operators

From pilot to operator?

Let's cut to the chase. You are a licensed pilot, but you want to up your game and become an operator.

Below is a SACAA table that appears on its website. It summarises the various authorisations that an operator needs to get going. But, as at May 2025, it is out of sync with the legislation on RPCs and RPLs. This table is copied everywhere on the web, without being updated, and is provided here as a warning more than anything else.

Required Approval	Commercial Operation	Corporate Operation	Non-profit Operation	Private Operation
ASL	Yes	N/A	N/A	N/A
UASOC	Yes	Yes	Yes	N/A
RLA	Yes	Yes	Yes	N/A
RPL	Yes	Yes	Yes	N/A
C of R	Yes	Yes	Yes	N/A
Note: RMT is required for maintenance on RPAS classified as class 3 and higher				

Abbreviations:
ASL – Air Service Licence
UASOC – Unmanned Aircraft Systems Operating Certificate
RLA – RPAS Letter of Approval
RPL – Remote Pilot Licence
CofR – Certificate of Registration
RMT – RPAS Maintenance Technician

What you, as a pilot wanting to become an operator, can get out of this table is the amount of paperwork that is involved in setting yourself up to fly drones not only as a pilot, but as an operator, in order to make money on a larger scale.

As at early 2025, 96 UAS operators are certified by SACAA: businesses (mapping, surveys, mining, forestry, commerce), universities, research organisations, flight schools, state agencies, the SABC, National Parks and conservation. The industry is very active.

Becoming an operator

If you want to become an operator, you have to follow procedures of approval or certification that are complex and thorough, always because of the risks posed by drones flying overhead, and losing control.

Becoming an operator involves a complex process, laid out in SA-CARS and SA-CATS **Part 101**. Often there will be a reference to a '**UASOC**' holder, which means an operator.

Here is the process that awaits you if you want to go from pilot to operator or UASOC holder:

Register each drone

You must register each drone you intend to operate, however: 'the receipt of the Certificate of Registration does not automatically confirm the right to possession of an RPA letter of approval'. Note 'RPA' for a UA, UAS or RPAS. It does not matter, but what does matter is that approval is not automatic. You'll find a copy of the form on page 94 (remember: only for drones that are not Classes 1A and 1B).

Obtain a Letter of Approval

It is also called a Letter of Authority, even Authorisation, acronym: **UASLA**. Regulation: 'A UAS shall not be operated within the Republic, unless such UAS has been issued with a UASLA by the Director'. '[A] UA must first be approved by the Authority for use by way of a UA Letter of Authority' – **for each drone**. A copy of a UASLA appears on page 98. It is valid for 12 months.

But first check the Safety System Register that SACAA continually updates. It is a register of 'approved' drones. Each one is given an **SSA** (Safety System Approval) number. See: https://www.caa.co.za/industry-information/airworthiness/#rpas-safetyassessment-register

If the drone that you would like to operate is not on the list, you must approach the manufacturer and ask it to apply for an UAS System Safety. The form is available on the SACAA website: CA 101-24 (Application for UAS system safety approval).

If your preferred drone is on the list, you can go ahead with your UASLA application.

Full documentation regarding design and safety

Prepare the documentation about the drone you want to use, as detailed and spelt out in SA-CATS 101.02.2 under UAS Safety.

Make provision for an altimeter

'Or equivalent', otherwise the concerned UAS can only be flown R-VLOS.

Be granted a certificate of registration

It will come with registration and nationality marks, abbreviated **CofR**: 'a UAs (!) must be registered by the Authority prior to use' – for each drone.

Apply for a UAS Operator Certificate or UASOC

Do so once the UASLA and the CofR are granted, and for each drone. There are two scenarios:

- if your intended operation is commercial, you must also apply for an Air Services Licence
- if your operation is corporate or non-profit, the Air Services Licence is not necessary.

A UASOC is valid for only 12 months, and renewal must be applied for 60 days ahead of the date of expiry. See page 100 for a copy.

Submit an Operations Manual

An Operations Manual must be submitted together with the UASOC application (laid out in detail in SA-CATS 101.04.5), 'including the manner in which each type of UAS and operation will be safely conducted'.

Submit a maintenance programme

A maintenance programme must be submitted for approval by SACAA 'for such UAS', acronym: **UASMT.**

Notify transfer of ownership

Notification must be done if applicable, and must be done for each 'concerned UA' within 30 days of the change of ownership.

In sum: The duties placed on a UASOC operator are specific and heavy, and listed in detail in the legislation: Part 101. SACAA has dedicated personnel to help you with the process: rpasInbox@caa.co.za.

So, if you decide to become an operator, you must think about it carefully. If you set up a business and employ people, a host of actions form part and parcel of your duties as an operator: ensuring the drones are per specs; training non-flying staff; storage, safety and security audits; management of documentation, records, flight folios and UASMT logbooks; securing insurance; and making sure that the pilots you contract are legit and observe all the requirements with regard to their licences.

It can be lucrative, however.

But you would leave the open-air world of flying drones for the air-conditioned world of managing drones.

We have nearly reached the end of this guide. You now know enough to get a drone and start flying privately with confidence, or to embark on the journey of becoming a licensed remote pilot with great career prospects, or to become a drone fleet owner.

But, last thing, let's fly over the border to get a sense of what happens in Botswana, Namibia and Zimbabwe!

Section 7

What about Botswana, Namibia and Zimbabwe?

In recent years our neighbours have developed their own legislation, which differs from that administered by SACAA. The notes below are not meant to repeat what has been covered about flying drones legally in the context of those three countries. It is just to make South African licence holders, or tourists travelling across our natural borders, aware that drones and bundu-bashing are not natural companions.

Botswana

Key rule: 'These regulations shall apply to all persons operating or maintaining a RPAS registered in Botswana wherever they may be and any RPAS operating in Botswana'. The Civil Aviation Authority of Botswana (CAAB) uses RPA and RPAS.

A drone cannot be operated in Botswana unless it is registered with CAAB. Bringing over a drone may be considered an import, and importation is subject to authorisation either through the vendor or by application. If it is a licence that matters to you, you can seek a validation (valid for 12 months) or a conversion of your South African RPC or RPL: the CAAB will examine if your RPC or RPL complies with their requirements for a 'remote pilot license' (no acronym) which, by and large, are similar to those for the South African RPC, while provision is made for B-VLOS 'internationally'.

There is no equivalent in Botswana to the South African private use of drones. Drones are classified into three categories – recreational and sports (A), private (B) and commercial (C) – and each category is sub-divided into three Classes by weight including payload (Class 1: 0–5kgs; Class 2: 5–25 kgs; Class 3: 25kgs+), with the result that all drone pilots need a remote pilot licence validated by the CAAB.

Operators must be Botswana nationals or residents.

If you pass these hurdles, here is the crunch, and it is worth quoting in full:

Art. 101(2)

'A person shall not use a remotely piloted aircraft to do any of the following

    (a) conduct surveillance of

        (i) a person without the person's consent, and

        (ii) private real property without the consent of the owner; and

    (b) photograph or film an individual, without the individual's consent, for the purpose of publishing or otherwise publicly disseminating the photograph or film:

Provided that, the photograph or film is for newsgathering or is taken at the events or places to which the general public is invited.

  (3) Infrared or other similar thermal imaging technology equipment fitted on remotely piloted aircraft shall be for the sole purpose of

    (a) scientific investigation;

    (b) scientific research;

    (c) mapping and evaluating the earth's surface, including terrain and surface water;

    (d) bodies and other features;

    (e) investigation or evaluation of crops, livestock, or farming operations;

    (f) investigation of forests and forest management;

    (g) investigations of vegetation or wildlife; or

    (h) investigation of other matters upon Authorization by the Authority.

Private use: 'A person shall not operate a RPAS for private purposes, unless with prior Authorization issued by the Authority and subject to the conditions as may be determined by the Authority. A private RPAS operations pilot shall be trained in accordance with training requirements as may be determined by [the] Authority.' What this training involves is not specified to date, but the issuing of a licence and the post-validation maintenance of competency when it comes to 'Private, Recreational and Sports Operations' are explicitly mentioned.

Recreational, an added layer: 'A sports RPAS operations for recreational and sports purposes shall be Authorized and conducted within a registered club which is approved by the Authority.'

Tourist: The CAAB has a tourist/temporary registration for your drone, which is an application for a RPA certificate, together with a security vetting application. But it will not exempt you from observing the rules.

The CAAB rules released in June 2024 are still being developed, but a framework has been in place since. By the looks of it, and given the extreme care taken in its overall structure, accuracy of wording and clarity, it is unlikely to change. It is actually a model of legislation.

Clearly, Botswana does not want its skies and landscapes being transformed into a free-for-all rodeo and pillaging.

CAAB contacts: info@caab.co.bw, caab@caab.co.bw Tel: +267 368-8200

Namibia

The Namibia Civil Aviation Authority (NCAA) has come up with a neat, handy and comprehensive flyer which, using a QR code, provides you with all the information that you need to 'operate', meaning 'fly', your drone in that beautiful country. One can't do any better than to reproduce it here – while being aware that regulations are dynamic so it is always safer to double-check with the issuing authority.

DO

- Keep Your distance at all times
- Be in possession of public liability insurance at all times
- Fly only during daylight
- Keep drone within your site at all times
- Only use one drone at a time
- Always check that your drone is in an airworthy state
- Think what you doing with any images as you may breach privacy laws.

GET PERMISSION

- From Namibia Civil Aviation Authority (NCAA) before operating a drone at all times
- From Namibia Film Commission (NFC) if you intend to make a movie
- From the Ministry of Environment, Forestry, and Tourism (MEFT) if you intend to fly in a National Park or Nature Reserve
- From owners of property you intend to operate your drone from

Commercial operations
Filming
Recreational use
Model aircraft
Surveys

RPAS

NCAA
NAMIBIA CIVIL AVIATION AUTHORITY

STEPS FOR FLIGHT

Register your Drone

Get a license or certificate

Get insurance

Apply for an operating approval

Scan this code for our RPAS application package:

Get in touch!

rpas@ncaa.na

Or Tel +264 83 235 2000

4 Rudolf Herzog Street
www.ncaa.com.na

APPLICATION PROCESS

For Namibian Residents:

1. Email rpas@ncaa.na for guidance
2. Register your RPAS
   - Complete an application form and pay fee
   - Submit customs certificate
3. Apply for certificate of competency
   - Obtain certificate of competency from an approved training organisation
4. Apply for an operational approval
   - Complete an application form and pay fee
   - Submit ID, insurance, registration, and certificate of competency

For Commercial Operations:

1. Email rpas@ncaa.na for guidance
2. Ensure your RPAS is registered and you have a certificate of competency as above.
3. Apply for a commercial operational approval, contact NCAA,
4. If you plan special operations you may need:
- For filming, approval of Namibia Film commission
- For operation over a national park approval from MEFT
- For survey operations, proof of registration as a land surveyor

Temporary approvals for non-Namibian residents:

1. Email rpas@ncaa.na for guidance
2. Apply for an operating approval
   - Complete an application form and pay fee
   - Submit copy of insurance and ID, registration, and competency if applicable
   - Submit declaration of flight zones (maps)

> "Drones are fun but they must be operated safely."

DON'T

- Don't fly over populated areas.eg. streets, towns and cities)
- Don't fly within 5NM (10 km) of any airfield/ aerodrome
- Don't fly higher than 45 meters (150 feet)
- Don't fly within 30 meters of buildings or structure, at sporting events, concerts and festivals
- Don't fly over vehicles where you may distract drivers
- Don't fly over personal property without consent
- Don't fly within published controlled airspace as well as restricted, prohibited, danger areas,
- Don't fly near or over military, police, or prison facilities

ABOUT NCAA

NCAA is responsible for safety oversight and regulatory compliance within the scope of all civil aviation activities, including all remotely piloted aircraft operations.

Fly Safe

Zimbabwe

In terms of regulations that were last updated in November 2022, if you want to fly your drone in Zimbabwe, remember the first rule: 'No person shall operate an RPA unless he or she is in possession of a valid remote pilot licence in the relevant category' (A, MR and hybrid VTOL) (on A and MR see page 48).

Your next step, and it is a big step, would be to get licensed, or to try to obtain a validation or conversion of your South African RPC to a Zimbabwean Remote Pilot Licence (although, according to the current application form, this is not an option). And you must be a national, a permanent resident or have a valid temporary work permit.

Note the hybrid VTOL category, specifically mentioned: it shows that the Civil Aviation Authority of Zimbabwe (CAAZ) is aware of the unique capabilities of this innovative technology with optimal relevance to agriculture, mining, mapping, search and rescue, and cargo. This will not be of direct importance to you on a sight-seeing visit, but it's a different story for operators.

On a visit you are likely to bring over your drone. But: 'No remotely piloted aircraft shall be operated within Zimbabwe, unless it has been registered by the Authority.' Do not use a drone belonging to a Zimbabwean friend, duly registered, if you are not licensed.

Some offences can lead to imprisonment up to three years, not to mention fines.

So, if you want to bring over your drone, read this first – my emphasis added:

Temporary importation of remotely piloted aircrafts

7. (1) No person may temporarily import a remotely piloted aircraft for the purposes of **private, corporate, non-profit** operations or **commercial** use unless that person—

    (a) applies for a pre-clearance approval to the Authority at least 30 days before the day of the temporary importation, stating the following information—

        (i) full name and address of owner or operator of the remotely piloted aircraft;

        (ii) country where the remotely piloted aircraft is registered and its use;

        (iii) model, serial number and manufacturer of RPA;

        (iv) weight of the remotely piloted aircraft;

        (v) specifications of the remotely piloted aircraft;

        (vi) purpose of the temporary importation;

        (vii) period of the intended temporary importation; and

        (viii) details of the place where the remotely piloted aircraft will be operated in Zimbabwe;

    (b) upon entry of the remotely piloted aircraft into Zimbabwe, obtains a temporary import permit from the Zimbabwe Revenue Authority.

  (2) A remotely piloted aircraft pre-clearance approval shall be valid for three months from the date of issue.

In short, **all operations** performed by an RPA brought over from our side of the border are subject to a **pre-clearance approval, including private flying** over your campsite. The legal age is 18.

As for the drones themselves, the classification of RPAS not only differs from that in South Africa but also, in Zimbabwe, even a light drone requires approval by CAAZ, while all the others must be registered.

Remotely Piloted Aircraft Classification Table

Class	MTOM (kg)	Document issued by CAAZ after registration
Class 1	Below 2 kg	Approval Letter
Class 2	2 – 7 kg	Certificate of Registration
Class 3	7 – 20 kg	Certificate of Registration
Class 4	20 – 70 kg	Certificate of Registration
Class 5	70 – 150 kg	Certificate of Registration
Class 6	Below 150 kg	Certificate of Registration
Class 7	Larger than 150 kg	Certificate of Registration
Class 8	Reserved	

H – means height above the surface

$Ek = 1/2*Mass *(1.4 \, vmax)^2$

What about setting yourself up as an **operator**? Here is a pointer, where we find criteria already encountered when we discussed 'commercial':

Operator certificate requirements

No remotely piloted aircraft operator shall operate a remotely piloted aircraft in terms of these regulations unless such person is the holder of—

(a) in the case of commercial, corporate and non-profit operations, a valid remotely piloted aircraft operator's Certificate (ROC) and the Operations Specifications attached thereto; and

(b) in the case of only commercial operations, an Air Services Permit issued in terms of the Civil Aviation Act [Chapter 13:16].

The CAAZ website is www.caaz.co.zw; contacts: pr@caaz.co.zw Tel: +263 (24) 258 500 920

Some Useful Forms and Documents

I have mentioned these throughout this guide. They are extracted from SACAA's public records, as all legislation should be. **They are for information only** and correct as at May 2025. **They have no legal value**, but they will give you a good idea of the details of the regulations and essential information that control drone flying.

RPC and RPL: The new terminology

SOUTH AFRICAN CIVIL AVIATION AUTHORITY	REPUBLIC OF SOUTH AFRICA CIVIL AVIATION AUTHORITY	SACAA Private Bag X 73 Halfway House 1685
Tel: (011) 545-1323 E-Mail: niemandj@caa.co.za	GENERAL NOTICE # PEL-2023/003 LICENSING Revision 1	DATED 26 March 2023

TERMINOLOGY CHANGES RELATING TO PART 71.

1. **APPLICABILITY**

This general notice serves to inform industry of the recently promulgated regulations relating to Remote Pilot Licenses.

2. **BACKGROUND**

Annex 1 Edition 14 references Remote Pilot License which is specific to RPAS operated in Instrument conditions internationally. With the availability of regulations, standards, and relevant supporting technology, RPAS operations are expected to begin integration by 2025 into controlled airspace with manned aviation. To enable a distinction between the types of RPAS operated within the South African airspace a differentiation between drone licenses issued was required.

Part 71 was originally separated from Part 101 but did not contain any amendments to support advancements within industry. ICAO issued a State Letter in 2018 proposing that a regulatory framework is developed to support International Instrument operations.

The Minister of Transport signed off the following regulations on 17 March 2023:
- South Africa has adopted a Remote Pilot Certificate for UAS operation defined under Part 71.
- Remote Pilot Licenses specific to drones operated internationally and within instrument flight conditions aligned with Annex 14 has been defined under Part 72

3. **PURPOSE OF THIS GENERAL NOTICE**

The purpose of this General Notice is to advise industry on the administrative changes that will be required due to the promulgated regulation relating to Part 71 and Part 72:
- All licenses issued as a Remote Pilot License under the previous Part 71 will be reprinted following a license renewal to reflect Remote Proficiency Certificate.
- All licenses issued as of 1 May 2023 under Part 71 will be issued as a Remote Proficiency Certificate.

4. **EFFECTIVE DATE**

This General Notice shall come into operation on the date of publication.

Issued by the South African Civil Aviation Authority (SACAA)		
Niemand	J NIEMAND	26 MARCH 2023
SENIOR MANAGER: PERSONNEL LICENSING	NAME IN BLOCK LETTERS	DATE

1

Discover the RPC syllabus (theoretical knowledge)

Extracts from SA-CATS Part 71, as from April 2023.

You will find the full document on SACAA website: open www.caa. co.za, follow Legal Information>Legislation then open Regulations>Civil Aviation Regulations, 2011, once on the Contents page, click on Part 71 RPAS Personnel Licensing>71.02.2, which will refer you to SA-CATS 71, click and the full details will be revealed. It is better to follow this route if you are not used to manipulating SA-CARS and SA-CATS.

4. RPC general examination
    4.1 The RPC general examination shall be passed before the first RPC category specific examinations may be written.
    4.2 The examination is not required for any subsequent RPC examinations.

5. RPC examinations
    5.1 RPC (A);
    5.2 RPC (H); and
    5.3 RPC (MR).

6. Items applicable to the remote pilot certificate general examination
    6.1 Air law for a UA in terms of Parts 71, 101 and Document SA-CATS 101.
        (1) Human factors –
            (a) Vision –
                (i) empty field myopia;
                (ii) adaptation to darkness;
            (b) autokinesis –
                (i) stress management;
                (ii) causes of stress (stressors); and
                (iii) signs and symptoms of fatigue;

    (c) Meteorology –
        (i) factors affecting air density;
        (ii) fog and mist;
        (iii) wind and gusts;
        (iv) thunderstorms; and
        (v) aviation weather reports;
    (d) Navigation –
        (i) latitude and longitude;
        (ii) aeronautical chart information (VFR); and
        (iii) GPS (Components of a GPS system as used on a UA);
    (e) Lighting for a UA.

(2) Items applicable to all RPC –

    (a) Construction and parts of a UA (as applicable to the category of RPC).

    (b) Forces acting on an aircraft (as applicable to the category of RPC) –
        (i) weight;
        (ii) lift;
        (iii) drag; and
        (iv) thrust.

    (c) Axes of an aircraft and motion about the axes –
        (i) lateral axis – pitch;
        (ii) longitudinal axis – roll; and
        (iii) normal axis – yaw.

    (d) Control of motion about the axes (as applicable to the category of RPC).

    (e) Propulsion systems (as applicable to the category of RPC) –
        (i) electric motors;
        (ii) Brushed motors;
        (iii) Brushless motors;
        (iv) Motor ratings;
        (v) Electronic speed controllers;
        (vi) Petrol engines;
        (vii) Fuel mixtures;
        (viii) Propellers and rotors;

   (ix) Sizes of propellers (length and pitch); and

   (x) Rotors.

 (f) Weight and balance (as applicable to the category of an RPC) –

   (i) dimensions and weight of a UA;

   (ii) arm, moment, reference datum, flight station, centre of gravity; and

   (iii) forward and aft limitations of centre of gravity.

 (g) Servo motors and servo actuators used in a UA.

 (h) Radio control link (C2 link) –

   (i) radio control transmitter and receiver;

   (ii) setup (as applicable to the category of RPC); and

   (iii) frequencies used.

 (i) Data link –

   (i) airborne receiver;

   (ii) remote pilot station –

    (aa) command and control functions;

    (bb) telemetry;

    (cc) detect and avoid uplink and downlink;

    (dd) first person view (FPV);

    (ee) mission planner software;

    (ff) position and obstacle mapping; and

    (gg) waypoint navigation;

   (iii) frequencies used; and

   (iv) setup.

 (j) Wireless links general –

   (i) line-of-sight;

   (ii) fresnel zones;

   (iii) interference;

   (iv) coverage range;

   (v) antennas as used in a UAS;

   (vi) flight controller (autopilot system) –

    (aa) inputs and outputs;

    (bb) inertial measurement unit (IMU);

    (cc) flight modes and facilities; and

    (dd) setup.

      (k) Batteries –
          (i) sealed lead-acid (SLA);
          (ii) nickel-cadmium (NiCad);
          (iii) nickel-metal hydride (NiMH);
          (iv) lithium-ion (Li-Ion);
          (v) lithium polymer (Li-Poly/LiPo);
          (vi) charging of batteries;
          (vii) Safety concerns; and
          (viii) Battery fires.

      (l) The functions and required actions of a UA observer.

7. Items applicable to the RPC (A)
    (1) The stall –
      (a) boundary layer;
      (b) stalling angle of attack; and
      (c) aeroplane characteristics at the stall.

8. Items applicable to the RPC (H)
    8.1 Flight controls –
      (a) collective control;
      (b) cyclic control; and
      (c) anti-torque control.
    8.2 Main and tail rotors –
      (a) swashplate;
      (b) rotor head;
      (c) rotor blade stall;
      (d) fly bar;
      (e) ground effect; and
      (f) helicopter setup.

9. Items applicable to an RPC (MR)
   Different configurations and frames

Read the RPC Skills Test

SOUTH AFRICAN

CIVIL AVIATION AUTHORITY

Section/division	Personnel Licensing		Form Number: CA 71-03.3
Telephone number	0860 267 435	Fax Number: 011 545 2520	
Physical address	Ikhaya Lokundiza, 16 Treur Close, Waterfall Park, Bekker Street, Midrand, Gauteng		
Postal address	Private Bag X73, Halfway House 1685 Email: ClientCare@caa.co.za Website: www.caa.co.za		

DETAILS OF BANK ACCOUNT FOR PAYMENT OF PRESCRIBED FEE

Bank: Standard Bank of SA Ltd	Branch: Brooklyn, Pretoria	Branch Code: 011245	Account Number: 013007971

COMPULSORY CLIENT PAYMENT CODE (to be completed on deposit slip)

Service/transaction	Over the counter payments	EFT, Internet, Wire, Electronic payments
Skill test report for PPL (A)		

SKILLS TEST OR COMPETENCY CHECK FOR REMOTE PILOT LICENCE AEROPLANE / HELICOPTER / MULTI ROTOR

NOTES:

1. This form must be submitted within 30 days of the completion of the skills test or revalidation, as applicable.
2. In the case of an initial skills test, this form must be accompanied by the application form CA101-01.0.
3. For this form to be accepted by the SACAA, each page must be completed in full and must be initialled by BOTH the examiner and the candidate with the exception of the signature page.
4. Any alteration to the test/check details, grading, observation(s) or any date must be initialled by the examiner. Any other alteration must be initialled by the candidate.

Initial skills test		Revalidation	

Details of Candidate

Surname		Initial(s)	
License Number		Phone number	

Test/check details

		Date of test 1 (dd/mm/yyyy)	
		Date of test 2 (dd/mm/yyyy)	
Examiner to check	Training certificate from manufacturer	Examination passed prior to test	
		Letter of recommendation (initial test only)	
	Licence	Logbook	

RPAS Type Training Course

Name of Course	
Organisation	
RPAS Type	
RPAS Weight	
Date of Completion	

RPAS Aeronautical Experience

	RPAS operating experience	Remarks
Enter hours		

Test/Check 1	Briefing Time		Flight Time		De-brief Time		Outcome	C		NC	
Test/Check 2	Briefing Time		Flight Time		De-brief Time		Outcome	C		NC	
Remarks											

CA 71-03.3		*11 OCTOBER 2023*		Page 1 of 6

Note to the examiner and candidate					
a.	Abbreviations				
C	Competent	**NYC**	Not yet competent	I	Initial skills test
R	Revalidation	✈	Mandatory aspect	**NA**	Not assessed

b.	A person is competent if he or she demonstrates a combination of skills, knowledge and attitudes to perform a task to the prescribed standard.
c.	Airmanship means consistent use of good judgement and well-developed knowledge, skills and attitudes to accomplish flight objectives.
d.	The candidate must demonstrate competency in all aspects of the ground evaluation section prior to proceeding with the practical test.
e.	The candidate may use all available automation and avionics unless otherwise specified by the examiner.
f.	The candidate shall use the standard operating procedures (SOP) and checklist applicable to the aircraft.
g.	When applying the following 4-point scale, the examiner must award the mark that best describes the weakest aspect(s) applicable to the candidate's performance.

EXPLANATION OF 4-POINT SCALE

4 = Excellent standard

Performance remains well above the minimum required standard.
- Aircraft handling is smooth and precise.
- Technical skills and knowledge exceed the required level of competency.
- Behaviour indicates continuous and highly accurate situational awareness.
- Flight management skills are excellent.
- Safety of flight is assured. Risk is well managed.

3 = Meets SACAA expected standards

Minor deviations from the minimum required standard occur and performance remains within prescribed limits.
- Performance meets the recognised standard yet may include deviations that do not detract from the overall performance.
- Aircraft handling is positive and within specified limits.
- Technical skills and knowledge meet the required level of competency.
- Behaviour indicates that situational awareness is maintained.
- Flight management skills are effective.
- Safety of flight is maintained. Risk is acceptably managed.

2 = Below SACAA expected standards

Occasionally, major deviations from the minimum required standard occur, which may include momentary excursions beyond prescribed limits but these are recognized and corrected in a timely manner.
- Performance includes deviations that detract from the overall performance, but are recognized and corrected within an acceptable time frame.
- Aircraft handling is performed with limited proficiency and/or includes momentary deviations from specified limits.
- Technical skills and knowledge reveal limited technical proficiency and/or depth of knowledge.
- Behaviour indicates lapses in situational awareness that are identified and corrected.
- Flight management skills are effective but slightly below standard.
- Safety of flight is not compromised. Risk is poorly managed.

1 = Not Yet competent

Unacceptable deviations from the minimum required standard occur, which may include excursions beyond prescribed limits that are not recognized or corrected in a timely manner.
- Performance includes deviations that adversely affect the overall performance, are repeated, have excessive amplitude, or for which recognition and correction are excessively slow or non-existent, or the aim of the task was not achieved.
- Aircraft handling is rough or includes uncorrected or excessive deviations from specified limits.
- Technical skills and knowledge reveal unacceptable levels of technical proficiency and/or depth of knowledge.
- Behaviour indicates lapses in situational awareness that are not identified or corrected.
- Flight management skills are ineffective.
- Safety of flight is compromised. Risk is unacceptably managed.

h.	Mandatory aspects may be waived if deemed unsafe or if not applicable to the aircraft in which the test is conducted.
i.	If the examiner selects **NA**, he or she must motivate the decision on the observations page.
j.	Should the candidate achieve a **2** in any aspect, he or she must be re-assessed **once** in that aspect during the same flight and the examiner must indicate the new grading (1, 3 or 4).
k.	This form will not be accepted if an aspect graded with a **2** is not re-assessed and re-graded.
l.	Should the candidate achieve a grading of **1**, in 4 or less aspects, he or she must undergo remedial training as prescribed in the SACAR and must be re-assessed **once** in those aspects using the same form. This form must remain in the possession of the ATO until a re-assessment is conducted.
m.	Should the candidate wish to be re-assessed by another examiner, the latter examiner shall liaise with the examiner who conducted the first test.
n.	Should the candidate achieve a grading of **1**, in 5 aspects, the test shall immediately be discontinued and the candidate must undergo remedial training as prescribed in the SACAR.
o.	The entire test must then be repeated using a new form. A copy of the old form shall be sent to the SACAA Testing Standards Section of the SACAA.
p.	The examiner must write comments on the observations page whenever an aspect is marked as **1**
q.	Should any aspect in sections **8** (Multi-pilot operation) or **9** (Airmanship) be assessed as "**NYC**", the entire test must be repeated using a new form and the examiner must send a copy of the old form to the Testing Standards Section of the SACAA.
r.	Typical areas of unsatisfactory performance and grounds for assigning a 1 are:
	1. any action or lack of action by the applicant that requires corrective intervention by the examiner to maintain safe flight.
	2. consistently exceeding the tolerances suggested below.
	3. failure to take prompt corrective action when tolerances are exceeded.
	4. doubt regarding the successful outcome of an aspect.
s.	The tolerances suggested below refer to transient and not continuous flight path excursions; allowance for turbulence must be made.

Recommended tolerances			
Aeroplane		**Multi-rotor/ Helicopter**	
Height	Within 10% of height above ground	Height	Within 10% of height above ground
Direction	Within 20 degrees of assigned direction	Direction	Within 10 degrees of assigned direction
Rate of direction change	Steady rate while maintaining height and steady bank angle	Hover stability	Stable hover with minimal control input within 1 meter radius
Take off	Stable after lift- off control inputs	Take off Stable lift- off with fixed directional control	
Landing	Stable approach with limited bank and pitch changes	Vertical Landing	Stable approach to landing area with a continuous descent on a nominated landing spot

CA 71-03.3	*11 OCTOBER 2023*	Page 3 of 6

Section 1: Ground evaluation

		Aspects		C	NYC
1	✈	CAR/CATS, AIP, SUPPLEMENTS, AICs, NOTAMs and completion of ATS flight plan			
2	✈	Interpretation of weather reports, forecasts and charts			
3	✈	Flight planning, aircraft performance and charts (SID,STAR, APP and en-route)			
4	✈	All weather operations			
5	✈	Technical knowledge of aircraft (POH, AFM as applicable)			
6	✈	En-route navigation preparation and preparation of IFR navigation log			

Section 2: Pre-flight Operations

		Aspects					
1	✈	Pre-flight inspection, take-off data, passenger briefing		1	2	3	4
2	✈	Pre-start, start and after start procedures	NA	1	2	3	4
3	✈	QNH set, flight instruments and navigation aids set and checked		1	2	3	4
4	✈	Taxi and aerodrome procedures	NA	1	2	3	4
5	✈	Take-off briefing (RTO, EFATO, DEP, and Threat mitigation)		1	2	3	4

Section 3: Take-off and climb procedures

		Aspects				
1	✈	Take-off technique (T/O roll, speeds, rotation, transition to instruments)	1	2	3	4
2	✈	Initial climb-out (speed and direction), after take-off checks and en route climb including altimeter setting procedures (if applicable)	1	2	3	4
3	✈	Climb profile	1	2	3	4

Section 4: Descent, Arrival and landing Procedures

		Aspects				
1	✈	Approach Pattern	1	2	3	4
2	✈	Quality of landing	1	2	3	4

Section 5: Flight Manoeuvres Items applicable to Aeroplane

		Aspects					
1	✈	Turns while maintaining altitude		1	2	3	4
2	✈	Speed changes while maintaining altitude		1	2	3	4
3	✈	Horizontal figure 8	NA	1	2	3	4
4	✈	Stalls	NA	1	2	3	4
5	✈	Spin recovery (if approved for type)	NA	1	2	3	4

Section 6: Flight Manoeuvres Items applicable to RPA Helicopter

		Aspects				
1	✈	Tail-in Hover	1	2	3	4
2	✈	Tail-in hover squares and circles	1	2	3	4
3	✈	Tail-in hover Horizontal figure 8	1	2	3	4
4	✈	Tail in hover vertical triangle	1	2	3	4
5	✈	Transition for hover to forward flight and back to hover	1	2	3	4
6	✈	Side on hover	1	2	3	4
7	✈	Nose in hover	1	2	3	4

CA 71-03.3	*11 OCTOBER 2023*	Page 4 of 6

Section 7: Flight Manoeuvres Items applicable to RPA Multi-Rotor

		Aspects				
1	✈	Tail-in Hover	1	2	3	4
2	✈	Tail-in hover yawing slowly right and left	1	2	3	4
3	✈	Tail-in hover moving right and left	1	2	3	4
4	✈	Tail in hover moving forwards and backwards	1	2	3	4
5	✈	Tail in hover climb and descend	1	2	3	4
6	✈	Tail in hover vertical rectangle	1	2	3	4
7	✈	Tail in hover horizontal rectangle	1	2	3	4
8	✈	Nose in hover	1	2	3	4
9	✈	Fly a square box rotating the MR in te direction of flight	1	2	3	4
10	✈	From hover fly a circle rotating the MR nose-in the centre of the circle	1	2	3	4
11	✈	Transition from hover to forward flight	1	2	3	4
12	✈	Climbing and descending from level flight	1	2	3	4
13	✈	Turns from level flight	1	2	3	4
14	✈	Speed control in level flight	1	2	3	4

Section 8: Abnormal / emergency procedures

		Aspects				
1	✈	Engine Failure after lift off	1	2	3	4
2	✈	Engine failure approach to landing	1	2	3	4
3	✈	Lost link	1	2	3	4
4	✈	Autorotation – if applicable	1	2	3	4

Section 9: Airmanship

		Aspects	C	NYC
1	✈	Situational awareness and safety consciousness		
2	✈	Use of checklist(s)		
3	✈	Event/risk management processes and aeronautical decision making		
4	✈	Flying skills, accuracy and smoothness		
5	✈	RT procedures and proficiency, ATC liaison / compliance		
6	✈	Compliance with regulations		
7	✈	Flight management (fuel, engine considerations, etc.)		

Observations

CA 71-03.3	**11 OCTOBER 2023**	Page 5 of 6

Details of examiner who carried out test			
Licence Number		Phone number	
I certify that all sections and aspects were carried out and assessed by me as indicated above			
SIGNATURE OF EXAMINER		NAME IN BLOCK LETTERS	DATE

Details of examiner who carried out re-test if applicable			
Licence Number		Phone number	
I certify that I re-assessed all the aspects as specified in the observation sheet			
SIGNATURE OF EXAMINER		NAME IN BLOCK LETTERS	DATE

I certify that this form has not been altered or tampered with in any way whatsoever and all information on it is correct		
SIGNATURE OF CANDIDATE	NAME IN BLOCK LETTERS	DATE

Application for the issue of an RPC

NO LEGAL VALUE, FOR INFORMATION ONLY

SOUTH AFRICAN

CIVIL AVIATION AUTHORITY

Section/division:	Personnel Licensing, Safety Standards and Assurance		Form Number: CA 71-03.2
Telephone number:	0860 267 235		Email Clientcaa@caa.co.za
Physical address:	Ikhaya Lokundiza, 16 Treur Close, Waterfall Park, Bekker Street, Midrand, Gauteng		
Postal address:	Private Bag X73, Halfway House 1685 Website: www.caa.co.za Email: ClientCare@caa.co.za		

DETAILS OF BANK ACCOUNT FOR PAYMENT OF PRESCRIBED FEE

Bank: Standard Bank of SA Ltd   Branch: Brooklyn, Pretoria   Branch Code: 011245   Account Number: 013007971

COMPULSORY CLIENT PAYMENT CODE (to be completed on deposit slip)

Service/transaction	Over the counter payments	EFT, Internet, Wire, Electronic payments
Fees: See CAR Part 187.00.23		

APPLICATION FOR ISSUE OF REMOTE PILOT CERTIFICATE
AEROPLANE / HELICOPTER / MULTI ROTOR

Notes:
1. See the relevant checklist on the SACAA (www.caa.co.za) for the applicable requirements for each licence or rating.
2. This form may be used to apply simultaneously for more than one licence or rating.
3. Insert a check mark (√) in the applicable box(es)*.
4. This form must be submitted within 30 days of the completion of the skills test or required training, as applicable.

DETAILS OF APPLICANT

Surname		First names		
License number (if applicable)		Date of birth		Age
ID/Passport number		Permanent resident in SA*	Yes	No
Training organization name		Training organization number		

QUALIFICATIONS

Tick the appropriate boxes below

PPL (A)	CPL (A)	ATPL (A)	PPL (H)	CPL (H)	PPL (H)
Restricted Radio Licence		Medical Class		English language proficiency level	

POPULATION GROUP* (for statistical purposes only)					GENDER*	
African	White	Coloured	Asian	Other	Male	Female

Nationality	
Residential address	

	Province		Postal code	
Postal address (if different)				
	Province		Postal code	
Telephone number		Cellular phone number	
Fax number		E-mail	

√ Application for category sort		√ Ratings *	
Remote Pilot License (A)		VLOS	
Remote Pilot License (H)		BVLOS	
Remote Pilot License (MR)		EVLOS	

SIGNATURE OF APPLICANT	NAME IN BLOCK LETTERS	DATE

CA 71-03.2	***25 AUGUST 2023***	Page 1 of 1

What you need to attach to your RPC application

SOUTH AFRICAN

CIVIL AVIATION AUTHORITY

Section/division	Personnel Licensing		Form Number: CA 71-30

REQUIREMENTS FOR APPLICATION OF RPC LICENCE

Date	
License Number (to be allocated)	

		TICK Y/N
ISSUE: CAR 101.03.1 (Skill test form must be submitted within 30 days of the skills test)		
1.	An applicant must be 18 years or older.	
2.	A certified copy of proof of identity / passport of applicant.	
3.	An application form must be completed.	
4.	Valid medical certificate class 4 for BVLOS or operations involving RPAS a class 3 medical certificate. issued in terms of part 67	
5.	Hold a restricted radio certificate of proficiency in radiotelephony(aeronautical).	
6.	English proficiency level 4 or higher.	
7.	Proof of written examination passed.	
8.	Have completed the flight training requirement at an ATO	
9.	Skills test form signed by an appropriate rated DFE/ Instructor	
10.	Letter of recommendation from ATO.	
4.	Two recent passport-size photographs of applicant.	
8.	Copy of the last 3 pages of logbook with a record of flight time	
9.	Outcome of test marked on the skills test.	
11.	Sign next to all amendments and no tippex allowed	
12	Appropriate fee as prescribed in Part 187	
Note:		

	R	
	Receipt number	

CA 71-30	*07 NOVEMBER 2023*	Page 1 of 1

The form says 'RPC licence'. It is meant to reflect a 'licensing' process. The RPC is a 'certificate' (see previous form), not a licence. But it makes you a licensed pilot.

Licensing fees

As at April 2025. Next increase: April 2026, and so on.

NO LEGAL VALUE, FOR INFORMATION ONLY

Fees as from 01/04/2025

STUDENT	FEE	FLIGHT ENGINEER	FEE
ISSUE	R 669	ISSUE	R 920
RENEWAL	R 575	RENEWAL	R 565
RE-ISSUE	R 669	RE-ISSUE	R 920
DUPLICATE	R 523	DUPLICATE	R 920
		RATINGS	R 450
PPL (A & H)		INSTRUCTORS RATING	R 711
ISSUE	R 868	**DESIGNATED FE**	R 680
RENEWAL	R 1234	**VALIDATION**	R 920
RE-ISSUE	R 868		
DUPLICATE	R 607	**CABIN CREW**	
VALIDATION	R 628	ISSUE	R 565
CONVERSION	R 931	RENEWAL	R 450
		RE-ISSUE	R 565
CPL (A & H)		DUPLICATE	R 565
ISSUE	R 931	RATING	R 429
RENEWAL	R 669	**VALIDATION**	R 868
RE-ISSUE	R 931	**CDE**	R 1443
DUPLICATE	R 920	**VERIFICATION LETTER**	R 680
VALIDATION	R 920		
CONVERSION	R 931	**RPL A & H & MR**	
		ISSUE	R 847
ATPL (A & H)		RENEWAL	R 617
ISSUE	R 1004	RE-ISSUE	R 847
RENEWAL	R 774	DUPLICATE	R 607
RE-ISSUE	R 1004	INSTRUCTORS	R 450
DUPLICATE	R 973	RATINGS	R 429
VALIDATION	R 994	**DRE**	R 941
CONVERSION	R 931		
		Class / Type Rating	R 450
FREE BALOON		**Night Rating**	R 450
ISSUE	R 868	**INSTRUCTORS**	R 711
RENEWAL	R 1234	**INSTRUMENT**	R 450
RE-ISSUE	R 868	**DFE A & H**	R 1904
DUPLICATE	R 607	**RTE**	R 1465
VALIDATION	R 617		
		EXEMPTION	R 3452
VERIFICATION LETTER	R680	**URGENT EXEMPTION**	R 8065

How to register a 'commercial' drone

NO LEGAL VALUE, FOR INFORMATION ONLY

SOUTH AFRICAN CIVIL AVIATION AUTHORITY	Department Telephone number: Physical address: Postal address:	AIRWORTHINESS: Aircraft Inspection & Registration **Form Number: CA 47-R1** 0860 267 435 Email address: registration@caa.co.za Ikhaya Lokundiza, 16 Treur Close, Waterfall Park, Bekker Street, Midrand, Gauteng Private Bag X73, Halfway House 1685 Website: www.caa.co.za

DETAILS OF BANK ACCOUNT FOR PAYMENT OF PRESCRIBED FEE

Bank: Standard Bank of SA Ltd   *Branch:* Brooklyn, Pretoria   *Branch Code:* 011245   *Account Number:* 013007971

APPLICATION FOR REGISTRATION OF REMOTELY PILOTED AIRCRAFT

Notes: (Please read carefully)

1. **Supporting documents:** the supporting documents to accompany each application are set out in detail on page 5. Please pay meticulous attention to compliance therewith.

2. **Certification of supporting documents:** Kindly note that certification of all annexures must be done by a Commissioner of Oaths or Notary Public of a **non-interested party** on the front of every page and must include a full signature and ink stamp with full details, address and certification statement of such Commissioner of Oaths or Notary Public.

3. The application plus all supporting documents must be submitted to the Director of Civil Aviation by emailing the documents to: registration@caa.co.za.

4. Where the required information cannot be furnished in the space provided, the information must be submitted as a separate memorandum and attached hereto.

1.	**PARTICULARS OF APPLICANT**			
1.1	Full name of the (Company, Close Corporation or Trust)			
1.2	Full Business/Residential Address		1.3	Postal Address
	Postal Code			Postal Code
1.4	Telephone Office		1.5	Telephone other
1.6	Fax Number		1.7	Fax Number
1.8	E-mail Address			
1.9	Legal status of Applicant (Company / Close Corporation / Trust)			
1.10	Registration number of Company / Close Corporation / Trust			
1.11	Date of registration of Company / Close Corporation / Trust			

CA 47-R1	30 August 2023	Page 1 of 4

1.12	Full Particulars in respect of each Director / Member / Trustee			
Surname & Initials	Position		Identity Number	Nationality

2.	**PARTICULARS OF AIRCRAFT**	
2.1	Current Nationality and Registration Mark of Aircraft (if applicable)	
2.2	South African registration letters, if registered previously in the Republic	z -
2.3	Manufacturer of the aircraft	
2.4	Manufacturer's model of aircraft	
2.5	Aircraft Serial Number	
2.6	Date of Manufacture	
2.7	Maximum Take-Off Mass (kg)	
2.8	Mark with an X the appropriate aircraft type, engine type & number installed, and the intended operation of the aircraft.	

Aircraft Type		Engine Type & Number Installed		Intended Operation	
Aircraft		Piston Engine 1, 2, 3, 4		Commercial	
Helicopter		Turboprop Engine 1, 2, 3, 4		Corporate	
Multi Rotor		Turbojet Engine 1, 2, 3, 4		Non- Profit	
		Electric 1, 2, 3, 4.			
		Other (Explain)			

2.9	Is the aircraft equipped with ACAS II, ADS-B and/or Mode S Transponder (if yes please submit CA91-12 form including the proof of payment)			
	YES		**NO**	
2.10	Please note that the receipt of the Certificate of Registration does not automatically confirm the right to possession of an RPA letter of approval.			

CA 47-R1		30 August 2023		Page 2 of 4

2.11	SUPPORTING DOCUMENTS
	Kindly mark and attach relevant documents and/or requirements

In the case of an RPA which is imported into the Republic for the first time or returns to the Republic and has to be re-registered on the South African Civil Aircraft Register (SACAR):

2.11.1.	An affidavit confirming the following: a) Non-registration or de-registration of the RPA from the State/territory from which the aircraft is imported b) Ownership of the RPA. c) Serial number of the RPA.	
2.11.2	A Copy of the Clearance Importation Document issued by SARS (Form SAD500), if not applicable, a confirmation letter from SARS as applicable.	

In case of ex-military RPA

2.11.3.	Confirmation issued by NCACC that the aircraft is not fitted with any armaments	
2.11.4	Registration fee as prescribed in Part 187	

INCLUDING REQUIREMENTS LISTED ABOVE

If the aircraft is to be registered in the name of a company:

2.11.5	a) A Copy of the latest register of directors approved in terms of the Companies Act, 2008 (Act No. 71 of 2008). (Form COR39)	
2.11.6	b) The authorizing resolution on pages 3 and 4 hereof	
2.11.7	c) Any of the following certified documents: SA identity document, SA passport, valid SA driver's license, as authorized on page 4 of the resolution	

If the aircraft is to be registered in the name of a close corporation:

2.11.8	a) A Copy of the latest founding statement approved in terms of the Close Corporation Act, 1984 (Act No.69 of 1984). (Form CK1/ CK2).	
2.11.9	b) The authorizing resolution on pages 3 and 4 hereof	
2.11.10	c) Any of the following certified documents: SA identity document, SA passport, valid SA driver's license, as authorized on page 4 of the resolution	

If the aircraft is to be registered in the name of a trust:

2.11.11	a) A Certified copy of the appropriate letter of appointment as trustee, issued by the Master of the High court. (Form J246).	
2.11.12	b) The authorizing resolution on pages 3 and 4 hereof	
2.11.13	c) Any of the following certified documents: SA identity document, SA passport, valid SA driver's license, as authorized on page 4 of the resolution	
2.12	I, the undersigned	
	(Full name of Director / Member / Trustee / Individual Authorised in the resolution on page 4 hereof to act on behalf of the applicant)	
	hereby declare that the above particulars contained herein as well as the documentation submitted in support of the application are true and correct in every respect and apply herewith for registration of the aircraft in the Republic of South Africa, onto the South African Civil Aircraft Register (SACAR).	

SIGNATURE OF APPLICANT	**NAME IN BLOCK LETTERS**	**DATE**
Capacity of signatory		
Name of Company, Close Corporation, Trust or other organisation		

CA 47-R1	30 August 2023	Page 3 of 4

RESOLUTION				
RESOLUTION OF THE				
	(Directors / Members / Trustees)			
OF				
	(Name of Company / Close Corporation / Trust)			
PASSED AT		*(PLACE)*	**ON**	*(DATE)*

RESOLVED:

3.	That		applies for
		(Name of Company / Close Corporation / Trust)	
3.1	the registration of the RPA on the South African Civil Aircraft Register (SACAR)		

Z		-				▮▮▮▮
Model						
Serial Number						

That	
	(Full names of the authorised individual)
Is authorised to take all necessary steps on behalf of	
	(Name of Company/ Close Corporation/Trust)

and to sign the application form and to finalise the application as specified above in execution of the resolution.

Signatures of AT LEAST THREE Directors/Members/Trustees

SIGNATURE	**NAME IN BLOCK LETTERS**	**CAPACITY**
SIGNATURE	**NAME IN BLOCK LETTERS**	**CAPACITY**
SIGNATURE	**NAME IN BLOCK LETTERS**	**CAPACITY**

CA 47-R1	30 August 2023	Page 4 of 4

Letter of approval for a 'commercial' drone

NO LEGAL VALUE, FOR INFORMATION ONLY

SOUTH AFRICAN

CIVIL AVIATION AUTHORITY

Section/division:	UNMANNED AIRCRAFT SYSTEMS
Telephone number:	011-545-1000
Physical address:	Ikhaya Lokundiza, 16 Treur Close, Waterfall Park, Bekker Street, Midrand, Gauteng
Postal address:	Private Bag X73, Halfway House 1685

Form Number: CA 101-01

e-mail: rpasinbox@caa.co.za

Website: www.caa.co.za

DETAILS OF BANK ACCOUNT FOR PAYMENT OF PRESCRIBED FEE

Bank: Standard Bank of SA Ltd   Branch: Brooklyn, Pretoria   Branch Code: 011245   Account Number: 013007971

COMPULSORY CLIENT PAYMENT CODE (to be completed on deposit slip)

Service/transaction	Over the counter payments	EFT, Internet, Wire, Electronic payments
Fees. See CAR Part 187.00.10		

APPLICATION FOR REMOTELY PILOTED AIRCRAFT SYSTEMS LETTER OF APPROVAL

Please mark the appropriate block

	Application for the issue of a RLA
	Application for a duplicate RLA
	Application for the amendment of a RLA

NOTES	i.	An application for the issuing of a RPAS LA must comply with the provisions of CAR 101.02.1
	ii.	Where the required information cannot be furnished in the space provided, the information must be submitted as a separate memorandum and attached hereto.

AIRCRAFT REGISTRATION MARKS   Z   -

1.   CONTACT DETAILS OF APPLICANT /ORGANIZATION

Name of applicant / organization / operator			
Organization/ /Operator's number			
Name of person responsible			
Telephone number			
Cell phone number		Fax number	
Position			
Date available for inspection		Location of Inspection	

2.   DESCRIPTION OF RPA

Manufacturer					Model designation				
Serial number					Date of manufacture				
Aeroplane			Rotorcraft			Multi-rotor			
						Number of rotors			

Classification	1A	1B	1C	2A	2B	3A	4A	4B
Maximum Take-off Mass				kg				
State/country of design								

3.   DESCRIPTION OF PROPULSION SYSTEM

Manufacturer			Model designation(s) if applicable		
Jet		Combustion		Propeller	Electric

4.   DESCRIPTION OF AUTOPILOT

Manufacturer		Model designation	
State/country of design			

CA 101-01	*06 February 2023*	Page 1 of 2

Software			
Version		Last updated	

5.	**DESCRIPTION OF REMOTE PILOT STATION**		
Manufacturer		Model designation	
State/country of design			
Serial number		Date of manufacture	
Software and version		Last updated	

6.	**PAYLOAD INFORMATION**		
Manufacturer		Model designation	
State of design			
Brief description			

7.	**ADDITIONAL INFORMATION/ATTACHMENTS**
Please attach the following documents.	
Note: Failure to attached these documents may negatively affect the approval of RLA	
Flight Manual	
Maintenance program	
Documentation as specified in Part 101.02.2 RPAS SYSTEM SAFETY	
RPAS proof of approval from ICASA	

8.	**DECLARATION**

I hereby declare that I am, or have applied to be, the registered owner (or the agent acting on behalf of the registered owner) of the aircraft described in paragraph 2 and to the best of my knowledge and belief, the particulars contained in this application are accurate in every respect and show compliance with Part 101 of the Civil Aviation Regulations, 2011, as amended.

SIGNATURE OF APPLICANT / OWNER / AGENT	**NAME IN BLOCK LETTERS**	**DATE**

FOR OFFICIAL USE ONLY			
APPLICATION ACCEPTED		**APPLICATION NOT ACCEPTED**	
File Reference		Proposed audit date	

SIGNATURE OF INSPECTOR	**NAME IN BLOCK LETTERS**	**DATE**
Proposed inspection date		

CA 101-01	*06 February 2023*	Page 2 of 2

Applying for certification as an operator

It says 'ROC' but the terminology has changed; it is a UASOC.

SOUTH AFRICAN
CIVIL AVIATION
AUTHORITY

NO LEGAL VALUE, FOR INFORMATION ONLY

Section/division	Flight Operations Department Part 101 Aerial Work	Form Number: CA 101-03
Telephone number:	011-545-1000	Fax Number: 011-545-1350
Physical address:	Ikhaya Lokundiza, 16 Treur Close, Waterfall Park, Bekker Street, Midrand, Gauteng	
Postal address:	Private Bag X73, Halfway House 1685	Website: www.caa.co.za

DETAILS OF BANK ACCOUNT FOR PAYMENT OF PRESCRIBED FEE

Bank: Standard Bank of SA Ltd	Branch: Brooklyn, Pretoria	Branch Code: 011245	Account Number: 013007971

COMPULSORY CLIENT PAYMENT CODE (to be completed on deposit slip)

Service/transaction	Over the counter payments	EFT, Internet, Wire, Electronic payments
Fees: See CAR Part 187.00.10		

PART 101 APPLICATION FOR ISSUE or RENEWAL OF THE REMOTELY PILOTED AIRCRAFT SYSTEM OPERATORS CERTIFICATE (ROC)

NOTES:

(i) This application must be signed by:

  (a) the holder of the air service licence, if a natural person;

  (b) each partner, if the application / notification is on behalf of a partnership; or

  (c) the officer(s) duly authorised to execute documents on its behalf, if the applicant / holder of an air service licence is a company, closed corporation or organisation, and must be accompanied by a certified true copy of the relevant authorising resolution

  (d) for corporate and non-profit operations, the Air Service Licence is not a requirement

(ii) Where the required information cannot be furnished in the space provided on this form, the information must be submitted as a separate memorandum and attached hereto.

(iii) All available space provided for answers on this form must be completed, if the space is not applicable, indicate with N/A.

(iv) The CAA reserves the right to not process the application at the operator's cost if all information is not provided and is not true and correct.

(v) All fields must be completed or crossed out unless otherwise specified.

(vi) Please allow a minimum of 7 days to process the application.

1. PARTICULARS REGARDING THE APPLICANT

FULL NAME OF OPERATOR	
TRADE NAME (if any)	
PHYSICAL ADDRESS	
	POSTAL CODE
CONTACT NUMBER	
E- MAIL	

2. LICENCE PARTICULARS (Tick applicable box)

PART	101			
ASL NUMBER(S)				
CLASS				

AIRCRAFT CATEGORY	A4	H1	H2					
TYPES OF AIR SERVICE	G1	G2	G3	G4	G5	G6	G7	G8
	G9	G10	G11	G12	G13	G14	G15	G16

3. APPLICATION PARTICULARS

Mark the appropriate block:

APPLICATION FOR THE INITIAL ISSUE OF A RPAS OPERATORS CERTIFICATE	
APPLICATION FOR THE RENEWAL OF A RPAS OPERATORS CERTIFICATE	

A. RPAS TO BE ADDED TO THE RPAS OPERATORS CERTIFICATE

No.	Registration	Weight (kg)	Category (A4, H1, H2)	Class	Make/Model	Fee
1.	ZT					R
2.	ZT					R
3.	ZT					R

CA 101-03	*15 NOVEMBER 2022*	Page 1 of 3

							R
4.	ZT						R
5.	ZT						R
6.	ZT						R
7.	ZT						R
8.	ZT						R

AIRCRAFT FEE	Total (1)	R
RPAS OPERATORS CERTIFICATE FEE (Initial & Renewal)	Total (2)	R
OPERATIONS MANUAL APPROVAL FEE (Initial)	Total (3)	R
	TOTAL (1)+(2)+(3)	R

B. REMOVAL OF RPAS FROM THE RPAS OPERATORS CERTIFICATE			YES	N/A
No.	Registration	Make/Model		Fee
1.	ZT			R
2.	ZT			R
3.	ZT			R
4.	ZT			R
REMOVAL OF AIRCRAFT FEE		TOTAL		R

C. PROOF OF PAYMENT ATTACHED	YES	N/A
GRAND TOTAL (A+B)	R	

4. AIRCRAFT DOCUMENTATION

The following aircraft documentation in respect of each aircraft required to be included on/added to the RPAS Operators Certificate as indicated above is valid *(Tick where applicable)*:

DOCUMENTATION (Please attach below)		YES	NO
1.	Radio Station Licence		
2.	Certificate of Registration		
3.	RPA Letter of Approval (RLA)		
4.	Insurance		
5.	Air Service License (If Applicable)		
Please note that if any of the above is not in place, the application will not be accepted/processed			

5. RPAS OPERATIONS MANUAL STATUS (APPLICABLE TO EXISTING ROC'S)

1.	RPAS Operations Manual (Name)	Revision Date	Revision Number
2.			
3.			
4.			

6. DECLARATION – SIGNATORY

For initial application:
*I/we hereby declare that *I/We are in possession of an Air Service Licence
*I/We may not operate the air service concerned contrary to the relevant manuals to be approved by the Authority and any provisions of the Air Services Licensing Act, 1990 (Act No. 115 of 1990), the Aviation Act, 1962 (Act No. 74 of 1962) and the Civil Aviation Offences Act, 1972 (Act No. 10 of 1972).

For corporate and non-profit organisation:
*I/We hereby declare that we may not operate the operating Certificate concerned contrary to the relevant manuals to be approved by the Authority and any provisions of the Air Services Licensing Act, 1990 (Act No. 115 of 1990), the Aviation Act, 1962 (Act No. 74 of 1962) and the Civil Aviation Offences Act, 1972 (Act No. 10 of 1972).

For approved certificate holder:
*I/We hereby declare that *I/We are in possession of an approved operations manual, that is up to date and that *I/We may not operate the air service concerned contrary to the relevant approved manuals and any provisions of the Air Services Licensing Act, 1990 (Act No. 115 of 1990), the Aviation Act, 1962 (Act No. 74 of 1962) and the Civil Aviation Offences Act, 1972 (Act No. 10 of 1972).

CA 101-03	**15 NOVEMBER 2022**		Page 2 of 3

NAMES, SIGNATURES AND CAPACITIES OF OPERATOR'S REPRESENTATIVES		
SIGNATURE AND *CAPACITY*	NAME IN BLOCK LETTERS	DATE
SIGNATURE AND *CAPACITY*	NAME IN BLOCK LETTERS	DATE
SIGNATURE AND *CAPACITY*	NAME IN BLOCK LETTERS	DATE

COMMISSIONER OF OATHS

I certify that the deponent(s) has / have acknowledged that he / she knows, and understand / they know and understand the contents of this statement, which was signed and affirmed / sworn to before me at

PLACE	on	*DATE*
Full Name		
Business Address		
Capacity		
Area		

SIGNATURE OF COMMISSIONER OF OATHS	NAME IN BLOCK LETTERS	DATE

CA 101-03	**15 NOVEMBER 2022**	Page 3 of 3

Application for drone filming in a South African National Park

Only the first two pages, to show you what a process it is. Go to the website www.sanparks.org to access the legal form.

APPLICATION FORM

South African
NATIONAL PARKS

For the use of <u>Remotely Piloted Aircraft Systems (RPAS)</u> / Drones / UAV's for <u>filming or photography</u> in areas managed by South African National Parks

APPLICATION COMPLETION PROCEDURES

- Application to be completed by the RPAS / drone pilot only (one per pilot).
- A production / event company may not apply on the pilots behalf.
- An incomplete or incorrectly completed application forms may result in application rejection or application delays.
- Note that fees are applicable to application and approval process.

1. APPLICANT

I/We the undersigned (the Applicant) _____ represented by (Full Names) _____ hereby apply for permission to pilot a Remotely Piloted Aircraft System (RPAS) / Drone in _____ National Park, managed by South African National Parks (SANParks) and understand that IF approval is granted, this will be subject to the conditions and regulations set out by SANParks and by the relevant Civil Aviation Authority (CAA) Legislation.

2. APPLICANT INFORMATION

Applicant / Pilot			
RPL - RPAS /Drone Pilot License Number		License Expiry Date	
Address			
Telephone Number			
Mobile Number			
Email Address			
Fax Number			

3. USAGE DETAILS

Kindly provide a brief description of the purpose for which this application will be used.

Event / Race / Production Title						
Type	Event	Function		Ceremony	Race	
	Film	Stills		Marketing Concessionaire		
Park / Location						
Flight Day(s)	Total Days			Start Date	End Date	
Flight Time	Total Duration			Time From	Time To	

Application form		Page 1 of 7

APPLICATION FORM

For the use of <u>Remotely Piloted Aircraft Systems (RPAS) / Drones / UAV's</u> **for** <u>filming or photography</u> **in areas managed by South African National Parks**

Setup Time	Start of set up to breakdown					

4. RPAS / DRONE USAGE DETAILS

LOCATION INFORMATION

Please the following details applicable to RPAS / Drone for which approval is requested.

Drone Registration Number	Type	Size	How drone is powered	Maximum Height	Minimum Height	Flight Time (Takeoff-landing)

Provide a detailed explanation of why a drone needs to be used for filming / photography.	
Provide a story board of what the drone would film / photograph. Please indicate if any animals, people or special effects will be requested as part of the shoot. Please see website for conditions around filming with animals and special affects.	
Indicate where the footage will be used: I.e. commercial, feature film etc	
Indicate where the drone(s) would be launched and land/ reflect Location on a map. Indicate parking on the same map	
Indicate flight path on a map	
Indicate how landing zone will be demarcated. (note no hazard tape may be attached to any SANParks infrastructure plants or trees.)	
Stipulate flight time for the drone(s) from take-off to landing	
What is the maximum distance the drone(s) will be from drone operator(s) / pilot(s), at any one time?	
Will the drone(s) be flown at more than 50m away from people at all times (including both horizontal and vertical heights)? Yes or No. If not, please explain	
Will the drone(s) be 50m from roads including road reserve at all times? Yes or No. If not, please explain	
Will the drone(s) be more than 50m away from buildings.at all times? Yes or No. If not, please explain	
Will there be any noise disturbance from the drone(s)	
Indicate Contingency plans for malfunction or poor weather conditions.	

Quick Reference Guide

A guide with a practical, no-nonsense approach is not the place to list books that one has read, or pretends to have read. But readers of this guide can be assured that I have done my homework. References, direct and indirect, to the legislative or regulatory framework in South Africa, reflect the up-to-date state of play. I have consulted numerous international publications, legal, technical, medical and scientific. I have extensively consulted reputable international sources – and checked shady ones, of which there are many, unfortunately, to see how misleading they can be.

Below is a list of useful, verified, reliable and freely available resources. Others, more specialised, have been cited along the way. The ones here are the most relevant. They are full of information and insights, and usually reflect, in their own area, where things stand with civilian drones. I provide links to the specific drone pages, to get you directly to what matters. Links to the civil aviation websites of Botswana, Namibia and Zimbabwe are given in section 7.

South African Civil Aviation Authority (SACAA)

https://www.caa.co.za/

To access the South African legislation in a version updated as soon as legal changes are 'gazetted' (officially published), rather follow this path because direct access to the legislation may be blocked:

home page www.caa.co.za>Legal Information>Legislation to view the Acts and Regulations as published by Lexis Nexis; once there, click on Regulations; then click on Civil Aviation Regulations, 2011; then click on Part 71 to read about RPAS Personnel Licensing / on Part 72 to read about Remote Pilot Licences / on Part 101 to read about Remotely Piloted Aircraft Systems.

These are the Regulations or SA-CARS; within them you will find links and references to the more detailed Technical Standards or SA-CATS.

You can also go to the SACAA summary 'Unmanned Aircraft Systems', but the legislation is the law, not the summary, as handy as it looks. Here is the link (in the hope that it doesn't move): https://www.caa.co.za/industry-information/uas/

International Civil Aviation Organization (ICAO)

https://www.icao.int/Meetings/DRONEENABLE2023Webinars/Pages/default.aspx

International Air Transport Association (IATA)

https://www.iata.org/en/programs/ops-infra/air-tragic-management/drones/

European Union Aviation Safety Agency (EASA)

https://www.easa.europa.eu/en/light/topics/drones

United States Federal Aviation Agency (FAA)

https://www.faa.gov/uas

United Kingdom Civil Aviation Authority (UK CAA)

https://www.caa.co.uk/drones/

Australia Civil Aviation Safety Authority (CASA)

https://www.casa.gov.au/drones

Transport Canada

https://tc.canada.ca/en/aviation/drone-safety

Acknowledgements

I spoke to many people in aviation as I wrote this guide. I need to specifically acknowledge Dr André Coetzee, Executive Chairman of Henley Air, and Mr Nicholas Mason (ATPL) also at Henley Air for generously sharing his insider's knowledge as an instructor; Ms Cindy Hendrikse, air traffic controller and one of my doctoral students, for giving me pointers; and Captain David Veyssière, French Aéronavale, for his friendship.

A special expression of gratitude goes to Mr Simon Thompson, formerly at the Law Faculty, University of Cape Town. When, five years after my *Air Law: A comprehensive sourcebook for Southern African pilots* (Juta & Co, 2019) was published, I went ahead, prodded by Juta's editors, to write this guide on drones, Simon studiously checked legal references I had used in 2019, now outdated, and even then somewhat uncertain. Simon's assistance was invaluable. He is now doing his Practical Vocational Training at Herbert Smith Freehills Kramer law firm in Johannesburg. Thank you, Simon.

Index

Page numbers in *italics* refer to tables and figures.

S

SACAA *see* South African Civil Aviation Authority

SA-CARS 4, 10, 57, 68, 105

SA-CATS 4, 57, 68, 69, 70, 81–84, 105

safety 12, 15

Safety System Approval (SSA) number 69

Safety System Register 69

SAMAA *see* South African Model Aircraft Association

scams 47

sea Remotely Operated Vehicles (ROVs) 7

Skills Test 57–58, 85–90

South African Civil Aviation Authority (SACAA)

    air law 4

    commercial flying 30–31, 33–34, 37, 39, 41–43

    forms 80–102, 105

    model aircraft 11

    operators 67–70

    private flying 13–14, 20, 24, 27

    RPC 45–47, 49–51, 54, 57, 59–62

    RPL 64, 66

    terminology 7

South African Civil Aviation Regulations *see* SA-CARS

South African Civil Aviation Technical Standards *see* SA-CATS

South African Model Aircraft Association (SAMAA) 10–11, 18, 27

South African National Parks *see* National Parks

spectacles 17, 51

spotters *see* observers

SRPL *see* Student Remote Pilot Licence

SSA number *see* Safety System Approval (SSA) number

Student Remote Pilot Licence (SRPL) 42, 65–66